Foundational structural analysis

abc Approximate Angle Height & Shape

Head & Foot or = Curved forms

Hooks = ½ of small O

Pen 'Lozenges'

Head may be Hooks OR Triangular

in ſ i j m n p r u

ARCHES

b h m n p r

&

(d u q) INVERTED ARCHES

(d u q) it resemble altered (both letters) but

starting ends ... arches some it

or x see pq *

* also be bo co pe ro &c.

the best way of treating opposing curves (receding forms) except in uncommon words & names *

alone or final

alone or with non-receding forms (as canvas) [but ovo]

sometimes

r with following letter

a b c d e f g h i j k l m n o

p q g h r s t u v w x y z & *

THE CRAFT OF
CALLIGRAPHY

ROMAN
CAPITALS

SQUARE CAPITALS
Pen made ROMAN CAPITALS
RUSTIC CAPITALS
a variety of square capital
UNCIALS
true pen capitals

roman half uncial
mixed uncial and cursive forms
Irish and English
founded on roman half-uncial.
half uncial
Caroline hand influence
caroline
by roman cursive

small roman   gothic

15th C. Italian writing became   In the 11th & 12th C.
the foundation of the small   curves give place
roman letter.   to angles.

small italic ITALIC CAPS.
mixed
roman and cursive
hand of the 16th C

VERSAL LETTERS

THE CRAFT OF CALLIGRAPHY

DOROTHY MAHONEY

PELHAM BOOKS
London

4428B – M Joseph – 30.10.85
Ref: 14266 – Mahoney
Bembo No 2 Roman – M14½, 10 on 11
CFD 2 – Floppy 372

First published in Great Britain by
PELHAM BOOKS LTD
44 Bedford Square
London WC1B 3DP
1981

Reprinted 1982, 1985

Mahoney, Dorothy
    The craft of calligraphy.
    1. Calligraphy
    I. Title
    7456'1   NK 3600

ISBN 0 7207 1365 X

Filmset and printed in Great Britain by
BAS Printers Limited, Over Wallop, Hampshire
and bound by Dorstel Press Ltd, Harlow, Essex.

Endpapers: Part of a postal lesson written by Edward
Johnston for Joscelyne Charlewood Turner. Reproduced by
kind permission of Mrs Joscelyne Charlewood Turner.

Frontispiece: DOROTHY MAHONEY An early, rough
unfinished sketch illustrating the development of manuscript
hands from the Roman capitals.

Illustration on page 6: Scribe sharpening his quill by
candlelight. A Rembrandt sketch, *circa* 1635, Weimar, from
Rembrandt – Master Drawings by Keith Roberts, published by
Phaidon Press, Oxford, 1976.

For Lizzie and Dick
and the twins,
Tom and Joanna

CONTENTS

ACKNOWLEDGMENTS

My thanks are due to the undermentioned who have most generously lent work for the illustrations: Ann Camp, Joscelyne Charlewood Turner, Heather Child, Sydney Cockerell, Sheila Donaldson-Walters, Alfred Fairbank, William Gardner, Clifford Hatts, Ann Hechle, Donald Jackson, John Lawrence, Alexander O'Sullivan, Joan Pilsbury, Roger Powell, John Prestianni, Gordon Ransom, Ieuan Rees, Vernon Shearer, Sheila and Julian Waters, Irene Wellington, Berthold Wolpe and John Woodcock.

I acknowledge with gratitude permission accorded by the following: Trustees of the British Museum, p. 25 (top), 70, 71, 74, 75 (inset), 82, 94 (left); Trustees of the Victoria and Albert Museum, 41, 83; The Art Museum, Princeton University and the Yale University Art Gallery, 21, 22, 23; The Merrion Press, 24, 25 (bottom), 77, 114 (top right); The Trustees of the David Jones Estate, 65 (bottom); Cheltenham College, 116.

My thanks are due to Priscilla Roworth for kindly allowing me to reproduce work from her father's *A Book of Sample Scripts.*

I am grateful, too, to my friend Roderick Whitfield for supplying a most interesting essay with illustrations for the section on Chinese calligraphy; to Clifford Hatts for photographing several manuscripts for the book; and to Eugène Press for his generous advice.

I owe very special thanks to past pupil and friend Marie Angel for her encouragement and criticism throughout the production of this book as well as for contributing work for the illustrations.

Finally, I am very grateful to my editor, Lesley Gowers, for her assistance and enthusiasm and for suggesting the book in the first place; to Patricia Walters, the book's designer; to Bob Eames for his advice on the jacket; and to Muriel Gascoin for guidance throughout.

DOROTHY MAHONEY
June, 1981

EDWARD JOHNSTON

A PERSONAL ACCOUNT

Had it not been for William Morris, founder of the Arts and Crafts Movement in 1888, and W. R. Lethaby, distinguished architect and friend of Morris, Edward Johnston might not have become the most influential calligrapher of our time. When, at the age of twenty-six, Johnston gave up his medical training in Edinburgh to study art, it was Lethaby who, with great perception, advised him to pursue his interest in lettering by studying the early manuscripts in the British Museum. Sydney Cockerell (later Sir Sydney Cockerell), who had been secretary to William Morris, was an authority on illuminated manuscripts and acted as Johnston's guide, pointing out the finest treasures in the Museum. Through his intensive researches Johnston discovered the methods and principles underlying formal penmanship and so became responsible for reviving the arts of calligraphy and lettering.

In 1899 Lethaby, then Principal of the Central School, London, appointed Johnston to teach lettering; and Johnston became the first teacher of lettering in England. Two years later, Lethaby was elected Professor of Design at the Royal College of Art and he inaugurated a lettering class at that college, again appointing Johnston as the tutor. Johnston's book, *Writing and Illuminating and Lettering*, published in 1906 and still the classic text book on the subject, had important repercussions in America, Australia and

A display card in red and black announcing a lecture on electricity with interesting experiments (Ditchling, *circa* 1912).

China, and in particular Germany.

I was privileged to be able to study lettering with Edward Johnston in my student days in the Design School at the Royal College of Art from 1924 to 1928. After a short break I returned to the College in 1932 as an assistant in Johnston's lettering class and when Johnston was absent I deputised for him.

Johnston's weekly lettering classes at the Royal College of Art were held in the Lower Design Room on the ground floor; Johnston wrote of it: 'I have a very big room with a great blackboard worked by pulleys, and a platform with a railing, where I stand or sit and look down on the seventeen embryo scribes below.' By 1924, when I joined the class, the numbers had increased considerably.

During his lectures Johnston made use of the great blackboard and wrote with broad

Four pages from my Johnston notebook, written (between 1924 and 1929) with double-pencils. *Above*: The angle, height and shape. Ratios constant in practice. The foundational hand.

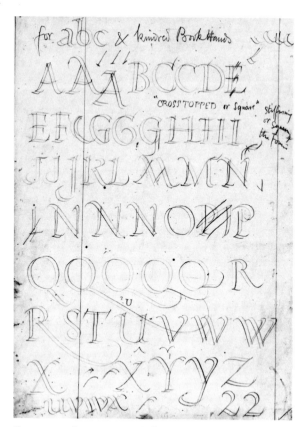

Cross-topped or square capitals.

chalks which were specially made for him. They were $4\frac{1}{2}$ inches long, 1 inch wide and $\frac{1}{2}$ inch thick. Johnston sharpened the chalks to a chisel edge, just like a pen.

When teaching he used the blackboard as a notebook – perhaps one week illustrating on it the characteristics of Roman capitals; the following week adding variations of serifs, heads and feet; the next week adding more varieties of shape, such as rounded capitals; and so on until the whole board was covered and he had to turn to a new page (clean the board).

Fortunately some of these blackboard demonstrations were photographed by Miss Violet Hawkes and can be seen (by special request) in the library of the Victoria and Albert Museum, London.

Sometimes Johnston would include in his lectures discussions on such topics as philosophy, mathematics, and his life-long search for Truth, with much going well above the heads of the average students. At other times his lectures were lucid and illuminated by his whimsical humour. For example, when criticising students' work he would ask if they knew the difference between a sculptor and a hairdresser, and explain that one makes faces

Branch-topped or round capitals.

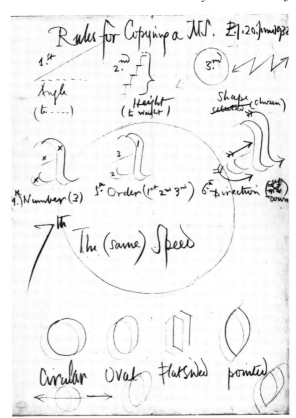

Seven rules for copying formal manuscript hands.

and busts while the other curls up and dyes, pointing out those of a student's letters which had 'curled up and died'.

To students who ruled double lines, he would say, *'Writing between ruled lines is like trying to dance in a room your own height.'*

Other Johnstonian precepts were:
'When in doubt use Roman capitals.'

'You cannot give a specimen of your writing any more than you can give a specimen of your smile.'

'Exaggerate or be normal.'

'A flourish is no good unless it flourishes, as cracking a whip is no good unless it cracks.'

'A rule is only a guide to ensure good work; having gained mastery by practice you should form your own rules.'

Johnston himself looked, and was, a frail man with a large and interesting head; his hands suggested the sensitive hands of a surgeon. He wore Harris tweed suits and his trousers were always baggy at the knees. Out of his pockets he would produce such items as knives, strips of tin, a magnifying glass, little slabs of ivory, string and double-pencils. These double-pencils were unique. Johnston loved making gadgets and by cleverly sliding a strip of metal between the two pencils he could adjust the distance between the two points from approximately ¼ inch to 1½ inches. This extreme difference between the two points enabled students to see clearly how 'weight' and 'height' influenced the form and shape of letters.

When Johnston's health declined, making journeys to London and teaching impossible, I was appointed tutor to the lettering class. This appointment lasted from 1939 to 1953, when Robin Darwin, then Principal, introduced typography and closed the calligraphy class. Sadly, many other schools of art followed Darwin's example.

I am happy to say that there is a resurgence of interest in calligraphy in England, America and on the Continent, but I regret that today's calligraphers lack the general training in the crafts and the arts of painting and sculpture considered essential for art students before the Second World War.

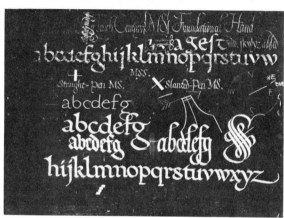

Two photographs of Johnston's blackboard demonstrations (1926–7), taken by Miss Violet Hawkes. These photographs illustrate the extraordinary control Johnston had over his broad chalks when writing on an old painted blackboard covered with irregular cracks.

Right: Greek uncials from Johnston's *A Book of Sample Scripts* (1914).

Requisition order in Johnston's handwriting for his lettering class at the Royal College of Art, 1930.

ΚΑΙΛΕΓΕΙ,
ΓΡΑΨΟΝ·ΟΤΙΟΥΤΟΙΟΙΛΟΓΟΙ
ΠΙСΤΟΙΚΑΙΑΛΗΘΙΝΟΙΕΙСΙ.
ΚΑΙΕΙΠΕΜΟΙ·ΓΕΓΟΝΑΝ.
ΕΓΩΤΟΑΚΑΙΤΟΩ,
ΗΑΡΧΗΚΑΙΤΟΤΕΛΟС.
ΕΓΩΤΩΙΔΙΨΩΝΤΙ
ΔΩСΩΕΚΤΗСΠΗΓΗС
ΤΟΥΥΔΑΤΟСΤΗСΖΩΗС
ΔΩΡΕΑΝ.ΟΝΙΚΩΝ
ΚΛΗΡΟΝΟΜΗСΕΙΤΑΥΤΑ,
ΚΑΙΕСΟΜΑΙΑΥΤΩΙΘΕΟС,
ΚΑΙΑΥΤΟСΕСΤΑΙΜΟΙΥΙΟС.·

A post card from Edward Johnston addressed to me.

Right: A New Year letter and a peace-offering cypher, with wedding congratulations to myself and my husband Charles.

Facing page: In 1916 Johnston was commissioned to design a special type for exclusive use by London Transport Services. His block letter or sans-serif alphabet, based on classical Roman proportions, was the forerunner of many sans-serif founts, including Eric Gill's for Monotype. The Johnston sans-serif had considerable influence in Germany.

ODBEFHIJKLMN

PQURSTVWCG

QU WA &YXZJ

Notes of details (in case of some being overlooked or in case of slight inaccuracies)
Note: the 2nd QU to be cut together on one key.

height of letters = 1″
width of stem = ⅟₇ th.
the curves of (B) are slightly less than ⅟₇ th.

OQCGS & are a little taller than 1″ and project slightly above & below top & foot lines.
J projects slightly below foot line
K top arm K & W, centre W, fall slightly below top line

WITH CARE, INK NOT waterproof.

obdcepqQUg as
aahijklmnrsek
tvwxyz   gg
1234567890
qupqjyg

The Scribe

What lovely things
Thy hand hath made:
The smooth-plumed bird
In its emerald shade,
The seed of the grass,
The speck of stone
Which the wayfaring ant
Stirs — and hastes on!

Though I should sit
By some tarn in thy hills,
Using its ink
As the spirit wills
To write of Earth's wonders,
Its live, willed things.
Flit would the ages
On soundless wings
Ere unto Z
My pen drew nigh:
Leviathan told,
And the honey-fly:
And still would remain
My wit to try —
My worn reeds broken,
The dark tarn dry,
All words forgotten —
Thou, Lord, and I.

ΥΠΑΡΧΕΙΘΕΟΦΙΛΕΙΓΕΝΕϹΘΑΙ

"... in that communion only, beholding beauty with the eye of the mind, he will be enabled to bring forth, not images of beauty, but realities (for he has hold not of an image but of a reality) and bringing forth and nourishing true virtue to become the friend of God and be immortal, if mortal man may."

Extract from Plato's 'Symposium' written in black on vellum in Greek uncials; a sharpened 'italic' and notes in a semi-formal hand. Johnston considered this one of his best manuscripts, and it was almost his last. It was given to Alfred Fairbank by the Society of Scribes and Illuminators in 1934.

Left: Johnston's 'The Scribe' by Walter de la Mare, especially written for me after completing my studies at the Royal College of Art in 1929. Written in a rich brown ink which Johnston mixed himself. Original size: 11 × 22 ins (280 × 560 mm).

CALLIGRAPHY

The word 'Calligraphy' is derived from Greek and means beautiful writing or penmanship. It covers many different modes of writing; for instance in Europe, since the Roman classical period, the term has been, and still is, used when describing manuscripts written for formal occasions, usually the work of professional scribes. The term is also applied to books, broadsides, etc. written in a cursive or running hand, i.e. Italic or Gothic cursive writing; and to beautiful contemporary handwriting written with a quill or metal pen.

In the East, the Chinese and Japanese esteem calligraphy and the calligrapher more highly than we do in Europe. There the brush is the tool of the craft, and handmade paper or silk are the writing materials for scrolls, panels, etc. The characters, ideograms, are executed with supreme skill, inherited from past generations of calligraphers.

CHINESE CALLIGRAPHY

The following notes on Chinese calligraphy by Professor Roderick Whitfield, Assistant Keeper of Oriental Paintings, Department of Antiquities at the British Museum, London, provide useful guidelines for students:

I have included an example of a standard script, in which each character is written in a square space (here actually ruled out) and each stroke of the brush is distinct. The characters are written from the top left corner of each to the bottom right corner, horizontals before verticals except when closing a box; the characters read in columns from top right to the bottom left. (All examples I have chosen are, of course, only parts of longer compositions.)

Structure and balance within the character is extremely important, and so is the articulation of the individual strokes. In this kind of standard script, the brush is held vertically and the course followed by the tip of the brush is kept hidden within the stroke, which has often a thickened end where the direction of the brush has been reversed to start or finish the stroke. In dots and hooks the tip can often be seen, of course.

The details from Huang T'ing-Chien's scroll dated 1100 are in a freer form of standard script. This is a monumental work with strokes and characters of great strength, and it would clearly be impossible to make this script conform to a ruled grid. Each character occupies a varying amount of space and there may be three, four, or five characters in a column. Successive strokes within a character are sometimes run together, and the writing is more direct than in the first example with fewer checks to the movement of the brush.

The poem by Yang Wei-Chen, in running-cursive, is still less formal. Not only are the strokes within each character run together, but commonly two or more characters are written continuously. There are still fewer checks and angles, and much more tonal variation as the brush's reserves of ink gradually dry and are then replenished.

When the ink is running dry the stroke may only skim the surface of the paper, revealing its texture. The writing is rapid and the course of the brush is easily seen even where a connection is not actually made explicit. Such an informal hand is more difficult to read and is used for drafts, letters between friends, and the like. Certain characters become abbreviated, as the strokes are run together, but the underlying structural sequence of strokes still enables similar characters to be distinguished one from another.

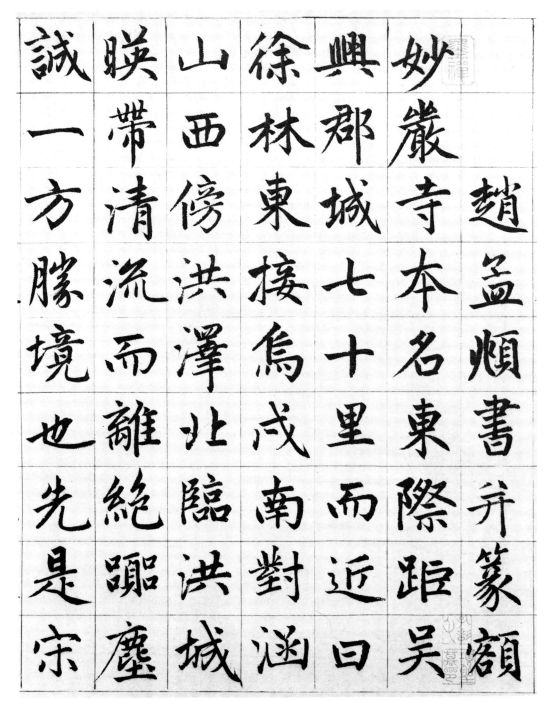

誠一方勝境也先是宗

暎帶清流而離絕塵

山西傍洪澤北臨洪城

徐林東接爲戌南對涵

興郡城七十里而近日

妙巖寺本名東際距吳

趙孟頫書弁篆額

Record of the Miao-yen temple in Hu-chou, written in medium standard script by Chao Meng-Fu (1254–1322).

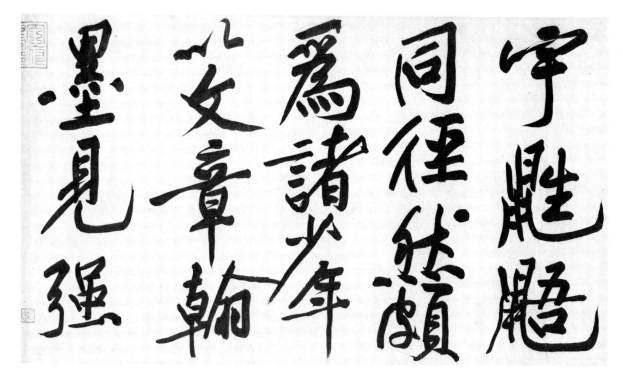

'Scroll for Chang Ta-t'ung', written in running standard script by Huang T'ing-Chien (1045–1105).

Right: Detail from the 'Scroll for Chang Ta-t'ung' by Huang T'ing-Chien.

Facing page: A poem entitled 'Drinking with My Wife Under the First Full Moon', written in running cursive script by Yang Wei-Chen (1296–1370).

咽生見恐圈此久
羹波別言圖此
羹言言圖亚雉
幸而起火辰涼蜀
言言言圖亚雉

ISLAMIC CALLIGRAPHY

The following introduction to Islamic calligraphy has been extracted from *Islamic Calligraphy*, published by the Merrion Press, London, 1976:

The Koran, which records the divine revelation to Muhammad, is the hub of Islam. Much of it was dictated to scribes by the prophet as it was being revealed to him. Because of this, many Muslims and some Islamicists have given Islamic calligraphy a sacred status, a judgment which has been supported by texts from the Koran itself. The introduction of printing in Islamic countries was often delayed by the prestige attached to the pen as the traditional instrument for recording God's word. As the Koran is known by heart, texts do not really have to be read but merely recognised; from the opening phrase of a 'sura' or chapter, the reader should know at once what follows. This means that the letters can be used to make very intricate patterns.

There are two main types of calligraphy. The earlier, 'Kufic', is distinguished by relatively square-shaped writing in straight lines across the page. Later came the various forms of rounded script, most particularly the 'Naskhi' hand and 'Thuluth', a script which gave special treatment to initial letters. Arabic is a cursive script running from right to left and was usually written with a reed on paper (which was brought to the West by Arabs).

The later scribes, particularly Turkish and Persian, enjoyed producing calligraphic conceits. They would repeat a phrase reversed mirrorwise, or perhaps play upon words, deliberately making puzzles to show off their skill.

FORMAL CALLIGRAPHY

Manuscripts written for important and special purposes such as royal, civil, ecclesiastical

Top: This stork, a holy bird, was drawn by a Mevlevi dervish, himself named after a stork. The drawing is a play on the dervish's name and that of his order's founder.

Above: An Islamic calligraphic pear design from the *Koran*; its contents translate as follows: 'In the name of God, the compassionate, the merciful.'

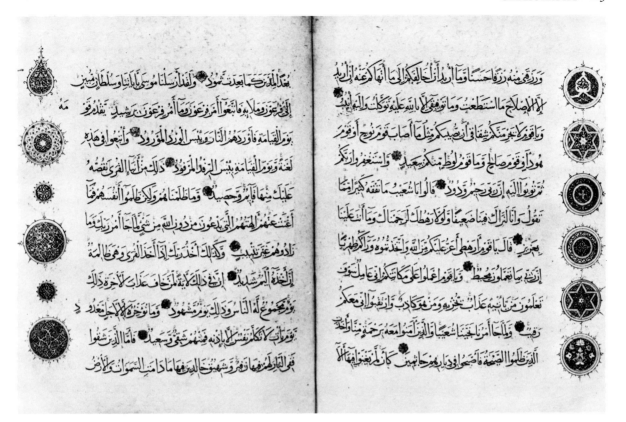

Pages from a 13th-century Arabic manuscript of the *Koran*.

Left: A circular design in which the name of Muhammed is repeated four times.

and military occasions, usually the work of one particular scribe or more, are called Formal Manuscripts. They may be written on papyrus with a reed, on vellum with a quill pen, or on paper (usually handmade) with a quill or metal pen.

These 'time-to-spare' hands are slowly and carefully formed with serifs, heads, hooks, feet, arms and often flourishes. Important words may be written large and in colour, the pages may be illuminated and often include gilding.

CURSIVE WRITING Cursive writing is the opposite of formal writing; it is a 'running' hand, or as Alfred Fairbank aptly says a 'no-time-to-spare' hand; it evolved from Roman capitals (*circa* 2,000 years old) rapidly scratched with a metal, bone or ivory stylus on to wax tablets, for everyday notes; the wax could be smoothed and used again. As we scribble reminders on a shopping-pad with a biro or felt pen, our handwriting is a very remote relation of the stylus-scribbled Roman Capitals.

Cursive writing, through speed, has shed all unnecessary strokes, so that changes have taken place in the form of certain letters. Letters are joined to each other by a thin oblique stroke, called a ligature, so that the pen writes as many letters as possible before being lifted, as though taking another breath.

TOOLS AND MATERIALS

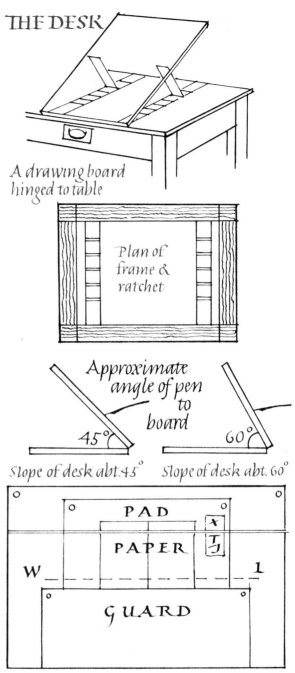

THE DESK

A drawing board hinged to table

Plan of frame & ratchet

Approximate angle of pen to board

45°   60°

Slope of desk abt. 45°   Slope of desk abt. 60°

PAD

PAPER

W ____ 1

GUARD

Pad under writing paper. Guard on which the hand rests. Tape to hold up the head of the manuscript. Paper, or vellum for trial stroke. W.L.= constant writing level.

THE DESK The calligrapher requires very few tools and materials compared with the book-binder, weaver, potter and silver-smith.

A basic requirement is a strong, firm table with a large drawing board hinged to the top to provide a sloping surface for writing. It is an advantage if the table has a drawer, in which pens, pencils, colours, brushes, ink, ruler, rag, etc. can be kept.

The simplest writing desk, or board, is made by hinging a drawing board, Imperial size, to the edge of the table and propping the board at the back by means of a wooden block or books.

Even better is an adjustable writing desk supported by means of a ratchet and strut so that the angle of the slope can be adjusted to suit the writer.

A portable board, often useful, can be made by hinging two boards together, or a board hinged to a wooden frame which has a ratchet and a strut is lighter to carry around. When no proper desk is available a board resting on the lap and against a firm table may be substituted but this restricts freedom of movement.

The table should be placed as close to the source of light as possible and any side light should fall from the left of the desk. A skylight gives a good general light. When writing by artificial light an angle-poise lamp on the left of the desk is best.

THE BOARD

It is better to write with a slightly springy pad under the writing sheet. A pad of two or three sheets of blotting paper or newspaper (ironed flat) covered with a clean sheet of white cartridge paper should be pinned on the board. Across the lower half or third of the board a sheet of stout paper, folded lengthwise, with the fold at the top, is pinned securely; this is called the 'guard' and on this the hand rests when writing. Near the top of the pad is stretched horizontally a strong piece of tape or elastic. The writing sheet, or paper, is slipped under this tape and beneath the guard so that it is securely held and may be moved up or down as the writer wishes. The 'writing level' is fixed at the most natural and convenient level for the writer, usually about an inch above the guard, and this level is always kept constant.

PAPER

The beginner may use any smooth unglazed white or cream paper; an unlined layout pad is suitable.

For the student who has acquired more experience a smooth handmade paper gives an added quality and value to the manuscript. Sadly, supplies of suitable cotton or linen handmade paper are very scarce and become increasingly expensive.

PARCHMENT

Parchment is sheepskin. Because of the oily nature of the sheep's wool, sheepskin has to undergo an entirely different method of processing from that applied to calf skin.

The greasy surface of parchment and the fact that one cannot erase without damaging the skin are reasons why I never recommend writing on parchment, although I believe Graily Hewitt★ always used it.

VELLUM

Vellum is a specially prepared calf skin, used chiefly by professional scribes. It should have a velvety nap, which is a perfect writing surface for the calligrapher and illuminator. The skin of a still-born calf has an even better writing surface because it is so soft and thin. It is excellent for small manuscript books but it is not always available.

Modern calf skins are treated with chemicals to speed up their processing but this tends to harden the vellum. The traditional method of washing, liming, scraping, stretching and pouncing took much longer but the resulting vellum was softer, as you can see by examining any medieval manuscript.

PREPARING VELLUM

I suggest that if the beginner wishes to use vellum, which is extremely expensive nowadays, he or she should seek the advice of a professional scribe, or join a calligraphy class so that the methods of preparing vellum for writing are thoroughly understood. A bookbinder could give helpful advice about the type of vellum suitable for a large or small manuscript book, the need for stitching and trimming the book and, above all, the correct arrangement of the pages and sections, the placing of hair side to hair side and flesh side to flesh side, throughout the book.

Pounce, finely powdered pumice or a combination of equal quantities of powdered pumice and powdered cuttlefish bone, is used to eradicate grease and other impurities on the surface of the calf skin. Powdered gum sandarac counteracts the slightly absorbent

★Graily Hewitt was an early pupil of Edward Johnston and later taught at the Central School of Art, London.

THE REED is cut abt. 8 inches long.
Cut off one end obliquely

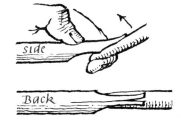

A brush handle is held under the nib, and is gently twitched upwards to lengthen the slit. The slit should be abt. ¾ inch long.

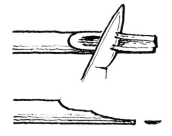

Shave away with a knife the soft inside part leaving the hard outer surface

The left thumb nail is pressed against the back of the pen – about 1 inch from tip – to prevent it splitting too far up.

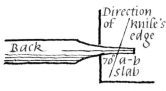

The nib is laid on the slab, back up, the knife-blade being vertical – the tip is cut off at an angle of abt. 70° to the shaft, removing the first rough slit. a→b

Place the nib back up, on the slab, & the knife blade being vertical, cut off the extreme tip at right angles to the shaft

Cut a strip of thin metal, very thin tin is good, cut the width of the nib and about 2 inches long. Make into a 'spring'

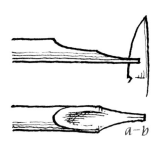

Make a short longitudinal slit a–b by inserting the knife-blade in the middle of the tip

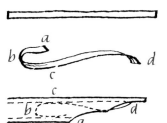

Insert the spring into the pen

The loop abc is 'sprung' into place & keeps the spring in the right position. The loop c d holds the ink & should lie fairly flat. The point d should be about ⅛ inch from the end of the nib

THE QUILL

shaft   barbs

A Turkey Quill is about 12 inches long, cut it down to 7 or 8 inches; a long feather gets in one's way.

The 'barbs' of the feather are stripped off the shaft

At one time it was possible to buy prepared quill pens which had a short slit, this could be lengthened to ½ or ⅜ of an inch. (see Reed pen)   Now we must make our own quill pens, first making a short slit & then lengthening it to ½ or ⅜ of an inch.

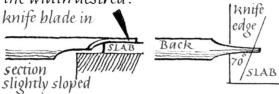

The shape of a bought nib   The shape of a pared nib
The sides of the nib are pared till the width across the tip is rather less than the width desired.

knife blade in

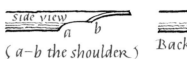

(a–b the shoulder)

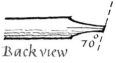

Back view   70°

The shaft is held lightly in the left hand, and the knife blade is entered with a steady pressure
The nib may be re-cut if it is not wide enough; if too wide, the sides may be pared down

Examine the nib with a magnifying glass, see that the ends of the two half-nibs are in the same straight line from the back and the under side

End   of nib
magnified

Nibs requiring recutting

under   under   back

Lay the nib, back up, on the glass slab, cut off the extreme tip obliquely to the slit, the knife blade being slightly sloped, & its edge making an angle of about 70° with the line of the shaft.

The Spring is placed abt 1/16 inch from the end of the nib. The long loop should be made rather flat to hold plenty of ink (A), not too curved (B) as this holds only a drop, nor quite flat (C)

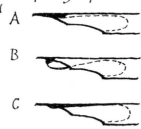

this draws the ink up and away from the nib

Nib for ordinary use

Nib for very fine stroke has a sharper angle

For large writing a broad nib

*Flattened in-
side gives a
full stroke*

Section of barrel of pen

Stroke

not flattened

*nib forms an arch
giving a hollow
stroke*

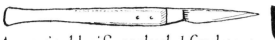

*A surgical knife, scalpel, I find very
satisfactory for quill-cutting. A fixed
stout blade is preferable to the fold-up
kind. Grind only on the right side of the
blade and taper to a point.*

surface produced by the pumice powder. It must be used sparingly otherwise the ink will retract to the top of the pen stroke and will not flow down again.

There are different methods of preparing vellum for writing. A skilled scribe might scrape down the entire surface with a very sharp knife.

A simpler method is to place on a flat surface a thick pad of newspaper covered with a sheet of clean white paper, and on this lay the vellum, hair side up. Then, using the palm of the hand in a circular motion, rub well all over some finely powdered pumice. Shake this off and sprinkle lightly with a little powdered sandarac.

If a manuscript is to be mounted, stretched and framed (a broadsheet) remember to write on the vellum before it is stretched. Gilding, however, must *always* be done after stretching, and any colour work too.

Vellum responds very quickly to variations of temperature: too much humidity in the atmosphere will make the vellum wrinkle and stretch; too dry an atmosphere will cause the vellum to shrink and harden.

Vellum manufacturers sell off-cuts which are most useful for practice. Beginners could try different pounces and a variety of skins, such as grained goat which has a darker tone.

PENCILS

Hard pencils are graded from H to 9H; soft pencils from B to 6B. Midway between are HB and F. For all ruling, a hard pencil is best; I like to use an H or HB on smooth paper, and a 7H on vellum because the skin has a soft surface. B pencils are useful when planning out and sketching drawn capitals and illustrations.

Double pencils or twin-points used in practice writing can be made with two HB pencils or one HB and one coloured pencil, preferably red.

A broad carpenter's pencil cut to a chisel edge is useful to simulate letters written with a broad-edged pen.

PENS

From earliest times a reed or quill has been used by scribes for formal writing. The present-day scribe or calligrapher uses a similar shaped reed, quill or metal nib and writes on a sloping desk just as the earliest scribes did.

Reed or bamboo pens are used for large writing. A beginner's first lesson could be to learn how to cut and use a reed pen. Quill pens are used for the smaller writing for MS books, broadsheets, notices. Nearly all professional scribes prefer the quill pen, especially when writing on vellum, since it is more flexible and sensitive than the metal pen.

Most turkey quills sold in art shops are poor in quality and expensive. To sharpen a quill requires expertise and patience and a considerable amount of wastage should be expected before mastering this skill!

The beginner might start collecting turkey quills from farmers and/or friends and keep the quills in a dry place for a year, after which they will be ready to use (naturally hardened). The largest wing feathers are best.

Turkey feathers are tough and are most commonly used; goose quills, which are softer and more pliable, are used for coloured versals and outline drawings; crow quills are used for very small writing and delicate outline drawings. Other birds' feathers you might add to your collection are seagull, swan, peacock and partridge.

Metal Pens Pens with metal nibs fall into two groups. The fountain pen with various interchangeable nib widths: fine, medium and broad; and the card with a pen holder which has a reservoir and twelve graded nibs, which can, if necessary, be sharpened. For the beginner I should advise the fountain pen (lettering set), because when the ink flows continuously one can concentrate on sitting correctly, holding the pen properly and following the form and construction of the letters.

The penholder with a metal nib presents certain difficulties. The nib in the penholder has to be 'fed' with ink from a brush held in the left hand. This may cause the pen to flood when it is charged with ink and the writing to become pale when the ink has run out. This could spoil the overall tone of the writing and present problems for the beginner scribe.

Posters and show cards require extra large

DOUBLE PENCILS OR TWIN POINTS

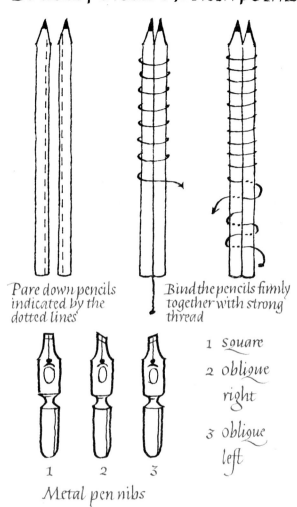

Pare down pencils indicated by the dotted lines

Bind the pencils firmly together with strong thread

1 square
2 oblique right
3 oblique left

Metal pen nibs

Fountain pen with six inter-change nib units

Metal pen nib with top reservoir in a pen holder

pens which are constructed to retain plenty of ink or colour. These plain stroke pens vary from $\frac{3}{10}$ inch to $\frac{3}{4}$ inch in width.

There are also other pens, such as border pens, edging pens and music pens, which are fun to use for greetings cards and for creating decorative all-over patterns.

INKS A good prepared liquid (carbon) ink is best for general use; this can be bought at most artist suppliers' shops such as Winsor and Newton, Rowney, Reeves or Rymans. These firms make their own inks and also supply other well-known inks suitable for calligraphy, such as Quink, Stephens, Swan and Watermans. In America the Pentalic Corporation, New York, supply everything for the calligrapher.

Most professional scribes prefer Chinese stick ink which does not clog the pen and gives a good jet black. To grind down the stick to make a liquid ink one can use Chinese or Japanese ink stones on which the ink is ground with a little distilled water. The liquid ink runs into a little channel (or well) in the stone made for that purpose. A small piece of plate glass (about 4 inches square with a ground glass surface) is an alternative but the liquid ink must then be transferred to a shallow saucer. Never allow the end of the ink stick to remain moist or the ink will dry and flake off. Always wash your ink stone and brush after use.

Non-waterproof inks should be used for all writing except for notices and posters for outdoor use. This is because non-waterproof inks are thinner and flow more freely than waterproof inks. Wash your palette, pen and brush thoroughly and frequently when using waterproof ink.

ADDITIONAL EQUIPMENT

Quill Knife For reed and quill cutting you will need a knife with a strong fixed blade, like a surgical scalpel. It should be ground on the right side of the blade and tapered to a point, and be kept very sharp.

Sharpening Stones You will need a fine and a coarse oil-stone and some good quality, thin lubricating oil.

Cutting Slab I find worn metal coins or a piece of celluloid satisfactory for cutting quill pens, and hard wood or bone suitable for reed or cane pens.

Magnifying Glass I like to have two magnifying glasses – one large one about $3\frac{1}{2}$ inches in diameter, and one small one about 1 inch in diameter. The large one is for examining several words or lines of manuscript; the small one for examining fine nibs.

Ruler A long ruler, of about 2 feet, with a metal edge is a great advantage. Dividers and compasses are also useful occasionally. A 'T' square is indispensable for ruling lines, especially when writing a book; a metal or ebony edge of a 'T' square could replace the metal edge of the ruler.

Brushes Two good quality sable-hair brushes, size '0' and/or '1'. One larger cheaper brush, to use with ink.

Cleaning Rag A clean rag, preferably cotton, for wiping pens, palettes and brushes is essential.

Bone Folder A bookbinder's bone folder, held in the left hand, will help to keep your writing paper flat and steady while you write. It is also useful when folding sheets of paper for a manuscript book or greetings card.

HOW TO USE A BROAD-NIBBED PEN

Before you start to write, check that you have all the essential tools and materials arranged on the left of the writing desk: pens, paper, pencils, paints, palettes, ink, brushes, knife, ruler, rag, etc.

A small piece of the same paper or vellum that you intend to use for the finished work should be pinned near the tape on the right-hand side of the board, for testing the nib width, its sharpness and the flow of the ink.

Never write with the board flat (horizontal) but have it raised to about 45°–60°, so that you can sit in a comfortable, upright position. The body and shoulders should be parallel to the writing desk so that the manuscript may be seen without any foreshortening; the forearms rest lightly on the writing board; the right hand holds the pen, the left the filler or brush.

When the board is raised to about 45° the pen shaft will be more or less horizontal; at this angle the ink will flow evenly. By elevating or lowering the board the ink in the pen will be made to flow more quickly or slowly.

The pen should be held lightly and easily in the hand: the thumb and index finger lightly gripping the shaft of the pen; the second finger supporting the shaft from beneath; the third and fourth fingers tucked into the palm; the side of the little finger and the palm resting on the board.

A rightly, not tightly, held pen should glide over the surface of the paper as a skater glides over the surface of ice. Most scribes hold the pen in the right hand, the left hand is then free to hold a brush or filler for recharging the pen when the ink runs out; holding the filler or brush in the left hand helps to prevent blots of ink from spoiling the manuscript.

When the pen is 'fed' with ink from the underside it is essential to see that the top side of the nib is kept quite dry. *Never* dip your pen into the ink bottle.

The pen should be held so that the chisel-ended nib is in perfect contact with the paper, both halves touching the surface of the paper. Pressing heavily on the nib will distort the letter form and damage the nib. The broad chisel-ended nib, properly used, will naturally make thick stress strokes the width of the pen, and fine hairlines at right angles to the thick stroke.

Wash thoroughly all pens and brushes after using and between work, and ink containers after a day's work. Special care is needed when cleaning pens which have been used with waterproof inks.

THE REVIVAL OF FORMAL PENMANSHIP

From his researches in the British Museum Library, Edward Johnston discovered that the broad-nibbed pen was the key to all formal writing or book hands in the Western world; and that scribes had used two methods of writing, which for convenience he called 'slanted pen writing' and 'straight pen writing'. Manuscripts written with the 'slanted pen' far exceeded those written with the 'straight pen', possibly because the majority of people had found it easier.

SLANTED PEN WRITING

Edward Johnston, to help his students at the Royal College of Art understand the difference between straight and slanted pen writing, devised a 'clock', divided into twelve equal parts and with thin pencil lines joined between 12–6, 1–7, 2–8, 3–9, 4–10 and 5–11. With a reed or broad chisel-ended pen held at a constant angle of 30° to the horizontal writing line the thickest stroke will be in a downwards direction along the 11–5 track; the thinnest stroke, upwards, along the 8–2 track. Naturally the other strokes will vary according to the directions, 12–6, 1–7, 2–8 and so on.

Rules for Slanted Pen Writing At first you may find it difficult to keep your pen at a constant angle of 30°. It will help if you rule lines at 30°, one or two inches apart, across your paper before beginning to practise your writing strokes.

The basic slanted pen strokes from which formal letters are constructed are formed as follows:
1. The thick oblique strokes follow the down track 11–5; the thin ones follow the 8–2 track.
2. The vertical strokes are produced downwards along the 12–6 track.
3. The horizontal strokes move from left to right along the 9–3 track.
4. The curved strokes, two half circles, spring from the top centre in a graduated arc to the left down to the lower centre of the O, and from the top centre in the opposite direction to the lower centre.

STRAIGHT PEN WRITING

Straight pen writing for most people makes for a difficult pen position because the thick stroke is vertical and the thin stroke horizontal, so that serifs and other terminal strokes require two or three additional pen lifts to complete each letter. Two of the most beautiful European book-scripts, however, are the Irish-Anglo-Saxon uncial and half-uncial developed by the monks of England and Ireland around the eighth century. These MSS are superb examples of straight pen writing.

With a reed or broad chisel-ended pen held at a constant angle of 0° to the horizontal line, the thickest stroke will be in a downwards direction along the 12–6 track; the thinnest stroke across from left to right along the 9–3 track, the horizontal line. Changes in the width of the other strokes will vary when the

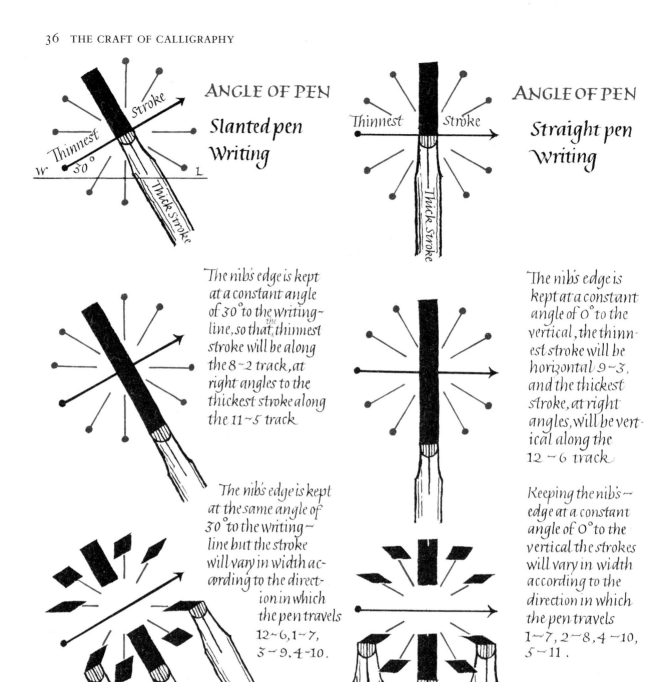

ANGLE OF PEN

Slanted pen Writing

Thinnest · Stroke · W · 30° · L · Thick Stroke

The nib's edge is kept at a constant angle of 30° to the writing-line, so that the thinnest stroke will be along the 8~2 track, at right angles to the thickest stroke along the 11~5 track

The nib's edge is kept at the same angle of 30° to the writing-line but the stroke will vary in width according to the direction in which the pen travels 12~6, 1~7, 3~9, 4~10.

ANGLE OF PEN

Straight pen Writing

Thinnest · Stroke · Thick Stroke

The nib's edge is kept at a constant angle of 0° to the vertical, the thinnest stroke will be horizontal 9~3, and the thickest stroke, at right angles, will be vertical along the 12~6 track

Keeping the nib's-edge at a constant angle of 0° to the vertical the strokes will vary in width according to the direction in which the pen travels 1~7, 2~8, 4~10, 5~11.

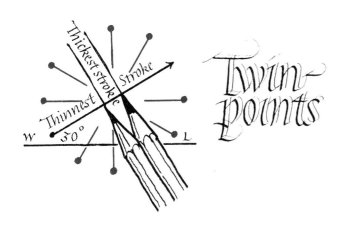

Twin-points

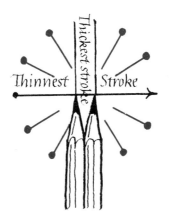

or Double-Pencils

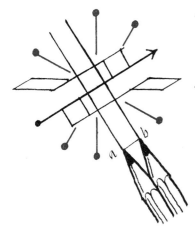

The Twin points are kept at the same constant angle of 30°

The points of the pencils correspond with the extreme corners of the broad nibbed pen (a—b)

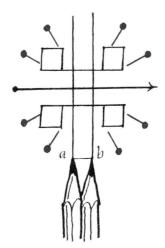

The Twin points are kept at the same constant angle of 0° to the vertical

The points of the pencils correspond with the extreme corners of the broad nibbed pen (a—b)

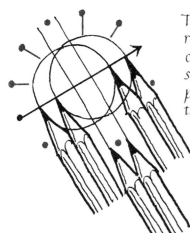

The pencil points represent a <u>square</u> cut nib ⚏ the shaft ▯ of the pen is in line with the thickest stroke

11—5

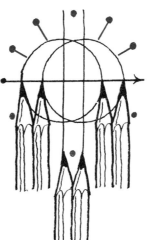

The pencil points represent a <u>square</u> cut nib ⚏ the shaft ▯ of the pen is in line with the thickest stroke

12—6

Basic strokes from which letters are constructed

Pen held at 30° to W.L..

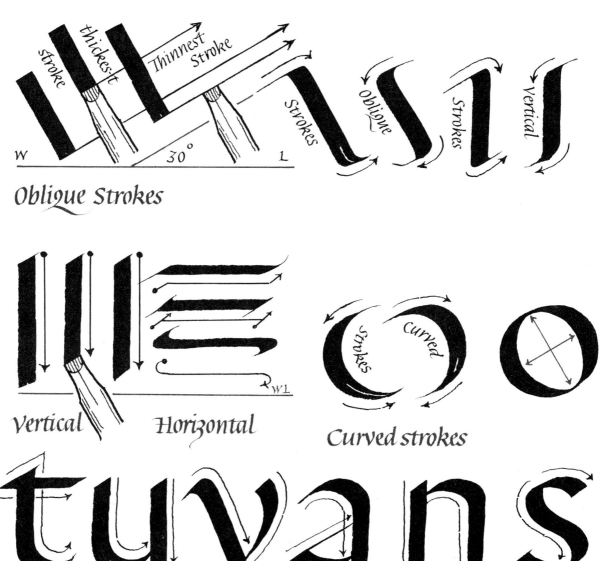

Oblique Strokes

Curved strokes

Vertical   Horizontal

Pen held at 0° to the Vertical

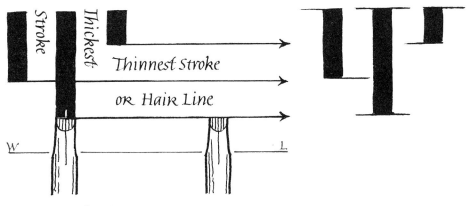

Vertical thick   Horizontal thin

Oblique strokes

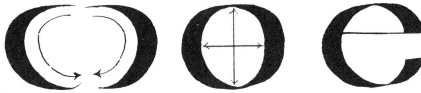

Curved strokes

pen travels along the 1–7, 2–8, 4–10 and 5–11 tracks. Notice that the slanted pen strokes in my 'windmill' suggest movement, the straight pen 'windmill' suggests static, classical qualities.

Rules for Straight Pen Writing The basic straight pen strokes from which formal letters are constructed are:

1. The pen is held at 0°. The thick stroke is vertical and the thin stroke, at right angles, horizontal.

2. The left oblique strokes start from the top at 10–4; the right oblique strokes from the top right downwards on the 2–8 track.

3. The curved strokes – two half circles form the O; begin at the top centre, execute first the left half and then the right. The 'O' is upright. Compare with the slanted-pen O which tilts to the left. Follow the direction of the arrow when you copy these strokes. The vertical, horizontal and oblique stroke shapes are written with a forward and a backward slide of the nib's edge.

ROMAN CAPITALS

Inscription from the Trajan Column (*circa* AD 114).

The Roman capitals of approximately two thousand years ago are the source from which all Western letter forms, capitals and small letters, written or printed, are derived. The form of the letters reflects the use of the tool that made them: a square-ended brush or reed pen, and the chisel, followed these strokes in the stone.

One of the finest and most renowned examples – although there are others of equally superb quality – is the inscription near the base of the Trajan column in Rome, AD 114. These capitals, called majuscules, are accepted as ideal letters for calligraphers to use as a model alphabet, because they are based on the simple geometrical forms of the square, the circle, the rectangle and the triangle.

Alphabets, like humans, have skeletons, and like humans, retain family characteristics. They vary in form and shape, openness or compression, lightness or weight, simplicity or exuberance. The relationship between body, head, arms, legs and feet must be in harmony with the character of any chosen alphabet. I would advise any student without previous knowledge of calligraphy to begin by studying and analysing the family relationships of the Roman capitals.

SKELETON FORM AND RELATIVE PROPORTIONS

In analysing the Roman capitals we find that the wide letters M and W fill the square or may be made a little wider than the square.

All curved forms are circular or are part of a circle: O and Q are complete circles; C, G and D are slightly less than a circle.

The rectangular letters, threequarters the width of the square, are H, A, V, N, T, Z and (U). They consist of vertical, horizontal and diagonal strokes, except U in which the verticals are linked by a quarter-circle arc.

K, X and Y can be thought of as 'double-decker' (two-tier) letters composed mostly of diagonal strokes. They look more comfortable and 'go with' the other letters if written five-eighths the width of the square.

The narrow letters, B, P, R and S, Johnston called 'double-decker' letters, B consisting of two small Ds, one on top of the other half the width of the square.

The other narrow letters, consisting of horizontal and vertical strokes, E, F and L,

 Round Letters 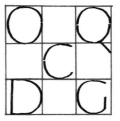 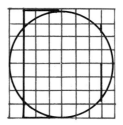 The skeleton form of the Roman Capital O & Q is circular, C.G.D are also circular but slightly narrower in width.

THE ESSENTIAL SKELETON

 Wide Letters 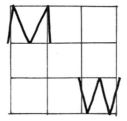 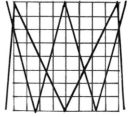 M & W are made a little wider than the square, OR the full width of the square.

FORM AND THE RELATIVE

 Rect ang ular Letters  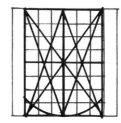 The rectangular letters HAVNTZ and U are three-quarters the width of the square.

PROPORTION OF THE ROMAN

 Letters 5/8 Width of square 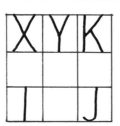 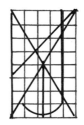 X Y K are about five-eighths the width of the square. The very narrowest are I & J. The hook of J is made from an arc of the small circle.

CAPITALS

 Narrow letters 1/2 width of square  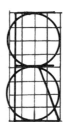 The narrow or double-decker letters, B P R S and E F L, are constructed from two squares, half the height & half the width of the full square.

ABCDEFGHI
JKLMNOPQ
RSTUVWXYz

Skeleton Roman Capitals written with a blunt point, or fine fibre tipped pen.

Roman Capitals written with twin-points.

ABCDEFG
HIJKLMN
OPQRST
UVWXYZ

Roman Capitals written with a square-edged pen.

cover the same area. The arms of E and F spring from the same point as the bows of the B, about the centre. The narrowest letters are I and J.

The key letters to any alphabet are O and I, and the calligrapher should be able to write a complete alphabet to match if given the weight, shape and characteristics of just these two letters.

When you have thoroughly studied the essential skeleton form and relative proportion of the Roman capitals, copy the diagrams with a black felt-tipped pen, biro, or sharp pencil (HB or B). Rule lines across your paper 1 inch apart (the letter height) with ½ inch between each writing line. First, write the letters in their respective groups (round, wide, rectangular and narrow), then write the letters individually, progressing to words and sentences when you feel ready.

The correct spacing of letters (even skeleton letters) is very important. Take care that vertical strokes are not too close, as the vertical rhythm of your writing is akin to the vital warp threads in weaving. They should be approximately the width of U or N apart in this particular alphabet.

The spaces between the letters are referred to as the inter-spaces, the spaces inside such letters as O, D, B and M, are referred to as counter-spaces. The subtle balance between inter- and counter-spaces is of great importance to the texture and rhythm of the whole page. It can be seen clearly when using double-pencils or a broad pen.

TWIN-POINTS OR DOUBLE-PENCILS

After practising the relative proportions of

the Roman capitals in skeleton form with a blunt point we come to the use of twin-points or double-pencils which simulate the broad-nibbed pen.

Twin-points are invaluable to the calligrapher: they are easy to prepare; can be carried about in the pocket or bag; do not leak as a pen might; may be used on any smooth surface anywhere, or on a book or pad; and are most useful when designing drafts for manuscripts or posters and the like. Johnston once wrote to me: 'I attach much value to the use of twin-points, and difficulties due to too dry corners are much more easily overcome (where you can see what happens) than by the wet nib, which tends to conceal one's faults.'

Difficulties in using twin-points owing to the tool being clumsy may be reduced in various ways, e.g. partly planing away both sides (or at least one side) of each pencil; wrapping in stout postcard and whipping cord firmly (but not too firmly) to prevent sliding.

The height (represented in nib widths) for the pen-written Roman capital is seven times the nib width (or, with twin-points, the distance between the two pencil points). To measure the nib widths hold your pencils with the writing edge vertical, mark off seven times the distance between the two pencil points making steps one above the other which just touch the previous stroke.

The twin-points and the broad-nibbed pen are held at an angle of 30° to the horizontal line for both Roman capitals and the small roman alphabet, this maintains the characteristics common to both families. Naturally, the shape and form of the letters will be changed by the pen width. The broad nib produces thick and thin strokes, adding flesh to the bones of the skeletons so that the physical appearance of the letters is changed considerably.

Round letters – O, for example – have a slight tilt to the left, and are wider across the 8–2 direction and narrower where the two halves of the circle intersect each other on the 11–5 axis; the counter-space inside the O is lemon like, pointed at the top and bottom. The other round letters follow the same basic pattern.

Because the broad nib adds weight, shape and form to the letters, we become conscious of the letter pattern against the background. Look at a page of the Roman round hand with its large open inter- and counter-spaces, and then compare it with the very compressed Gothic script. You will notice quite different textural effects. The abstract 'warp' pattern of the Roman H, I and J is the key to the general rhythms of the Roman hand when vertical strokes come side by side, like warp threads in weaving.

Evenness of texture is a desirable quality in lettering, and to preserve this evenness the space between two vertical strokes is furthest apart; a straight and curved stroke, or curved and straight stroke, is a little nearer; two curved strokes still closer; and the distance between letters, the inter-space, should approximately balance the counter-space.

For fun, enjoy a little freedom with your twin-points. Take a sheet of paper, rule across lines about 2–3 inches apart at the 30° angle; the only 'must' is that the pen's edge should be held at the 30° angle, so skate freely in any direction you like.

USING A BROAD PEN

Writing with a broad-nibbed pen is not as easy as writing with twin-points. One must learn to feed the pen with ink, and prevent blobs (of course if you use a fountain pen this difficulty is obviated).

Use a wide-nibbed pen to begin with because the form of the letters is more pronounced. Before beginning to write with the pen, the writing paper should be ruled, with narrow margins on either side. Measure seven nib widths, just as you do for the twin-points, and allow half the letter height between each writing line. For beginners it may help if lines at 30° to the horizontal line are drawn across the writing lines so that the pen hold can be checked constantly.

Do not grip the pen, let it glide easily over the surface of the paper. Keep both halves of the pen edge in contact with the paper. Pressing on the pen spoils the nib edge and stiffens and distorts the form of the letters.

Begin by copying the basic letter strokes for the slanted pen: oblique, vertical, horizontal and curved. Continue by writing the round, wide, rectangular and narrow letters, checking the number, order and direction of the strokes, then progressing to words and sentences.

Aim to produce clarity and regularity, which in turn produce legibility, a most desirable quality for any calligrapher to achieve.

The skeleton Roman capital alphabet we have studied is geometrically constructed; when we write with the broad-nibbed pen the eye demands greater subtlety of form, distinctiveness and character. B, P, R and S are aesthetically more pleasing if the upper bow is slightly smaller than the lower bow. It follows that the horizontal cross strokes of E,

F and H coincide with the junction of the bows of B, P and R, just above the centre; the tail of K and R spring from the same position, or a little below. A on the other hand has its crossbar lowered so that the upper triangle balances the lower part.

Letters of the same width (H, N and U) are connected by horizontal, diagonal and curved strokes. M, V and W have strong stress strokes. Q may have a simple tail or a curved flourished one. The letters X and Y have their junctions slightly above centre or a little below. However, do not worry if an understanding of these finer distinctions takes time and practice to achieve.

SERIFS   Serifs or finishing strokes terminate the direction of a stroke. A vertical stroke is terminated by a short horizontal stroke, or by a triangular head which acts as an effective optical termination.

SPACING   The spacing of letters in a word, words on a line, and writing lines to the text column are of vital importance to the calligrapher. The letters, the counter- and inter-spaces, the ribbon-like texture of the writing line weaving across the text column, set the pattern for the whole manuscript.

Capitals may be written one writing line apart, or a half or a third of the letter height apart; much depends upon what you are transcribing and which script is applicable, massed, fairly open or very open.

EDWARD JOHNSTON'S RULES FOR COPYING

Now study carefully Edward Johnston's

SPACING
Counter and Inter–spacing; Letters, Words and Lines

II QUILL
Keep two straight strokes furthest apart

IO MONK
A straight & curved stroke a little closer,

OO BOOK
and two curved strokes still closer

THE SPACE BETWEEN
WORDS IS THE WIDTH
OF AN 'O'

LINES OF CAPITALS
WRITTEN ONE LINE
SPACE APART

LINES OF CAPITALS
HALF LETTER HEIGHT
APART

MAN BY HIS REASON–
ING POWER CAN ONLY
COMPARE AND JUDGE
OF WHAT HE HAS AL–
READY PERCEIV'D

Serifs or Finishing Strokes
A serif terminates the direction of a stroke, a vertical stroke is finished with a short horizontal stroke or triangular beak or head.

I E H R

Cross-Topped Serif 'a'   *Triangular 'Head' 'b'*   *Curved Serif 'c'*

ABCDE
FGHIJK
LMNOP
ORSTU
VWXYZ
M N

Curved serifs may be used on diagonal strokes V.W.X.Y. & A; the tails of K & R may also finish with a curved serif

EJ's Seven rules for Copying Formal Writing

These Seven Rules apply when copying any kind of Formal Manuscript Hand.

The following guide generally applies only to the Roman Capitals and the roman small letters or minuscules.

The CHARACTER of the writing is determined by three factors, the Weight, Angle and Shape.

Weight

The number of nib·widths in relation to the height of the letter.

Position of pen when measuring the nib·widths.

Angle

The angle of the nib's·edge in relation to the horizontal line.

For this particular hand the pen is held at approximately 30° to the W. L.

Shape

The shape of the curved letter 'O' and the finishes of the straight strokes, i.e. 'I'

O I

'O' is approx: circular 'I' is finished with an horizontal cross-stroke.

Three factors affecting the CONSTRUCTION of the letters. Number, Order and Direction of Strokes.

Number
Order &
Direction
of Strokes

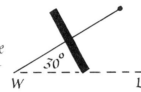

& Speed which combines all six factors.

seven rules for copying formal writing, applied to the Roman capitals.

THE THREE FEATURES WHICH DETERMINE THE CHARACTER OF THE WRITING ARE:

Weight	Seven nib widths.
Angle	30° to the horizontal line.
Shape	O is circular; I has a horizontal cross stroke, above and below.

THREE FEATURES AFFECTING THE CONSTRUCTION OF LETTERS ARE:

Number of strokes	Number of separate strokes in each letter.
Order of strokes	Order in which the strokes are written in each letter.
Direction of strokes	Direction in which pen travels in making each stroke.
Speed of writing	A fast script, cursive italic cannot be written slowly, nor can a slow finished hand, like half-uncials, be written quickly.

SMALL ROMAN LETTERS

Small Roman letters or minuscules, often referred to by typographers as lower-case, evolved from Roman capitals rapidly scratched with a stylus on wax tablets, as we would use a scribbling pad. From these cursive capitals the small letters gradually developed.

The essential difference between Roman capitals and small letters is that capitals are uniform in height whereas small letters could be said to be written between four lines; o and other letters such as a, c, e, m, n, s, u, v, w, x and z have bodies; b, d, f, h, k and l have bodies and ascending strokes; p, q, g, j and y have bodies and descending strokes. The pattern made by the small letters is like a ribbon running across the pages with the ascenders and descenders forming a fringe on either side.

The circular O which dominates all curved forms in the capitals also dominates the curved forms in the small Roman alphabet. The 'weight' of the small letters is four nib widths; that of the letters with ascenders and descenders, seven nib widths (three nib widths for the ascenders and descenders).

The distance between the writing lines is three 'O' spaces, so that ascenders and descenders should not touch.

Notice that the arcs of the circles in h, m, n, and b, t, u, spring from the vertical stem. They may be visualised as Roman arches, the stems of the columns supporting the arch.

Study the small letters as you did the

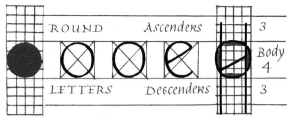

THE SKELETON FORM

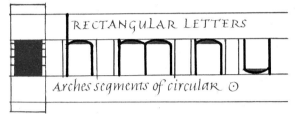

& RELATIVE PROPORT~

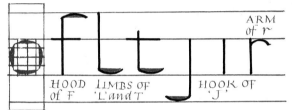

1ON OF THE SMALL

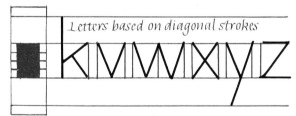

ROMAN ALPHABET

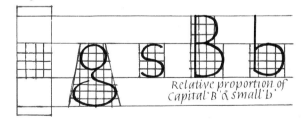

abcdefgh

Skeleton form of small roman letters

ijklmno

written with a blunt point or felt pen.

pqrstuv

Numerals to go with the Roman capitals

wxyz&12

and small roman letters: written

34567890

between two parallel lines, or, with even

123456789

numerals a little taller and the odd

ones a little longer .

abcdef g

Skeleton small roman letters written with twin-

h ij k l m n

points showing the method of construction.

o p q r s t

The Number, Order, Direction of strokes

u v w x y z

Triangular   Head or
O ⌐ 1 h   Heads   Foot Hooks

abcdefghij

A ROMAN LOWER-CASE ALPHABET TO GO WITH

klmnopqrs

THE PEN-WRITTEN ROMAN CAPITALS

tuvwxyz &1

1. WEIGHT Four nib widths

2. ANGLE 30° with the horizontal line

3. SHAPE 'O' is approximately circular

roabcde

abcdefghyk

fghijklm

lmnopqrstu

nopqrstu

vwxyz &123

vwxyz &

4567890&123

capitals; first in skeleton form in its various groups, then with twin-points without adding the finishing strokes, and finally the complete alphabet with serifs, triangular heads, hooks and feet.

NUMERALS Numerals to match the Roman alphabet should be the same texture as the writing; if mixed with capitals they may be the same height, if accompanying small letters, about the height of t. They may be written between parallel lines, or with the even numbers a little taller and the odd numbers a little longer.

DESIGNING A MANUSCRIPT BOOK

If you have followed these instructions carefully it should now be possible for you to write out a favourite short piece of prose or even begin a simple book.

A simple manuscript book offers the novice calligrapher or professional scribe the best means of combining practice with a most useful form of training in many aspects of lettering and design. To make a manuscript book we must first be quite certain about the kind of book we wish to write; whether it is to be a large, medium or small book will doubtless be determined by its purpose. Will it be:

1. A book for a child?
2. A student's note book or a diary?
3. A book to lie on a table or to be held in the hand?
4. A book to be carried in the pocket?
5. A book to be read in a church or other public building?
6. A book for ceremonial occasions, i.e. a wedding or baptism?

SIZE AND SHAPE
Next, decide the size and shape of the book. Take a sheet of the paper you would like to use, preferably a smooth-surfaced paper, fold it carefully into two pages and crease the spine with a bone folder. If the paper curves over and stays down by its own weight it is suitable; if the paper stands up it is too thick and unsuitable for a book. (See illustration.)

A sheet of paper, or vellum, folded once is called a *folio*; folded twice to form four leaves, *quarto* (4 vo); folded three times it becomes an *octavo* (8 vo), having eight leaves or sixteen pages.

A section normally consists of four book sheets, eight leaves, or sixteen pages. If the paper for the book is thin the section could consist of eight folded sheets, placed one inside the other to make a section of sixteen leaves, thirty-two pages.

A single-section book, as the name implies, is one such section; a multi-section book has several sections which are stitched together and attached to strong boards by means of tapes or cords.

It is a useful rule for the beginner to keep to three set sizes of manuscript book – *large*, folio size; *medium*, quarto; *small* octavo – and to use pens suitable for the three sizes.

WIDTHS OF MARGINS
The margins of a manuscript book follow more or less the proportions of those found in medieval manuscripts, occupying about three fifths the area of the page. The ratio of the margins is $1\frac{1}{2}$ (inner) : 2 (head) : 3 (outer) : 4 or 4+ (foot). Therefore, when viewing two facing pages (a 'double-page spread') the text areas are separated by three units of equal width; the remaining margins are multiples of this unit in the ratio given above.

The margins of a book are as a frame is to a

How to select suitable paper for a manuscript book

Take a sheet of paper you would like to use for your book & cut it exactly the same size. Fold it carefully into two pages and crease it with a bone folder along the spine. If the paper curves over & stays down by its own weight it is suitable.

If the paper stands up it is too thick.

Planning a single section book.

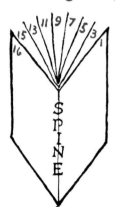

A section normally consists of four book sheets, eight leaves or sixteen pages.

p 1·2, 15·16 End papers
p 3 Title·page
p 5 Beginning of Book.
p 12·13 End of Book.
p 14 Colophon

All downward measurements taken from the Top cut edge, all horizontal measurements from the spine outwards.

a. Top or 'Head' of book, a cut edge
b. Deckle may be left on foredge and foot of Book.

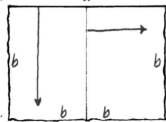

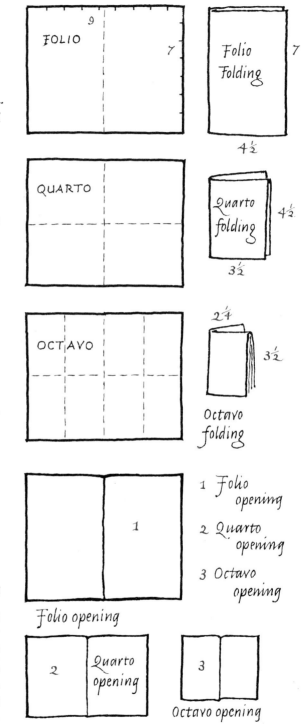

FOLIO
9
7

Folio Folding
7
4½

QUARTO

Quarto folding
4½
3½

OCTAVO

2¼
3½
Octavo folding

Folio opening
1

1 Folio opening
2 Quarto opening
3 Octavo opening

2 Quarto opening

3 Octavo opening

painting, they prevent the eye from wandering off the page. A narrow head margin is reasonable because the eye travels down the page. The widest margin, at the foot, allows room for the hand to hold the book without damaging the text, and is aesthetically pleasing in that it prevents the text column from appearing to fall through the bottom of the page.

Edward Johnston offered the following formula to his students if they had difficulties in setting on the margins:

For the common folio and octavo, with page proportions $7:4\frac{1}{2}$

make $\begin{cases} \text{height of text column} & = \text{width of page} \\ \text{width of text column} & = \text{two fifths height of page} \end{cases}$

For quarto

make $\begin{cases} \text{unit of measurement} & = \text{one sixteenth} \\ \text{for margins} & \text{height of page} \end{cases}$

Personal adjustments may be made for books for special occasions: the margins may be wider, the text columns smaller; or, for books of notes, diaries or records the text column area could be larger and the margins smaller.

If you are planning a multi-section book leave a little extra margin all round: on the inner margins, to allow for the stitching, and on the head, foredge and foot for trimming to size by the bookbinder.

SIZE OF WRITING
The distance between the writing lines when the small roman hand is used is three times the 'o' height, this just allows ascenders and descenders to clear each other (as shown in my diagram).

The distance between writing lines for Gothic scripts which are angular and very compressed is commonly two 'o' spaces, but between the lighter flourished italic hands five or six 'o' spaces, depending upon the length of the ascenders and descenders.

The average number of words to a line of manuscript is approximately six to eight, and the average number of letters in an English word is five or six, so if you allow the width of an 'o' between each word, the approximate number of letter spaces to a line would be 35–45. Naturally, if a very compressed hand is used, the number of letter spaces to a line would be increased.

When the 'o' height has been settled the space between the writing lines can be established. If the interline spaces do not exactly fit into the text column area it is possible to encroach on the inner or foot margins.

The ruling should be done lightly with a very hard pencil. The vertical marginal lines are ruled first, from head to foot of the page; the horizontal lines are ruled afterwards, the first and last horizontal lines are ruled straight across the double-page spread. It makes ruling more accurate if the paper or vellum sheet is kept flat and the verso (left) and recto (right) pages are ruled at the same time.

RULING
To facilitate the ruling of the pages a paper or vellum scale is an accurate method of ruling and a quick one too. Using exactly the same vellum or paper that the book will be written on, cut a strip $1\frac{1}{2}$ inches deep, and, if possible, wider than the double-page spread. Rule a line down the centre of the strip. On one side mark the vertical

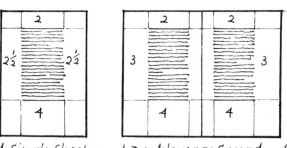

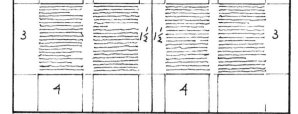

A Single Sheet *a*   A Double-page Spread   *b*   Oblong book: with double columns *c*
or Broadside   Upright book

Proportions of Margins for (a) Broadside: (b) Upright M.S. Book : (c) Oblong M.S. Book

	2 HEAD MARGIN			2 HEAD MARGIN	
FOREDGE MARGIN 3	Length of Text Column (1–13)	INNER MARGIN	INNER MARGIN	←Width of Text Column→	FOREDGE MARGIN 3
	FOOT MARGIN 4	1½	1½	FOOT MARGIN 4	

VERSO   RECTO

1 2 3 4 5 6 7 8 9 10 11 12 13

SIDE MARGIN	HEAD MARGIN	TEXT	COLUMN	FOOT MARGIN	
←SIDE MARGIN→	←WIDTH OF TEXT COLUMN→	INNER MARGIN	INNER MARGIN	←WIDTH OF TEXT COLUMN→	←SIDE MARGIN→

marginal lines, and on the other, mark the horizontal marginal lines – head, text columns and foot margins. This scale rule should be made carefully and accurately and can be used for all page measurements throughout the book. (See illustrations.)

PLANNING A SINGLE-SECTION BOOK

A single-section book consists of four sheets, eight leaves, sixteen pages (see illustration). The physical structure of a single-section book is as follows:

End papers or fly-leaves – one or more leaves of the first and last pages of the book. A book of any size and importance would have three or four end papers at the beginning and end of the book. End papers protect the manuscript and constitute margins for the body of the book.

The top edge of a book should always be a cut edge. If a handmade paper is used the deckle edge could be left on the foredge or foot of the page, but although it may look nice it does attract the dust. It is common for a multi-section book to have a gilt top to prevent the dust from penetrating into the book.

Top margins throughout the book are kept at exactly the same level; any irregularity at the top of the page catches the eye at once. Edward Johnston illustrated this point to me by sketching a clothes line: all the clothes hung from the same line but the garments were of very different shapes and sizes (see illustration).

The title page, as its name suggests, has the title and the author's name on it. Its spacing and arrangement should be linked with the inter-line structure of the book and the text column area. Capitals are most frequently used and colour too with decoration. The title page is usually a recto page and the titling is generally placed in a symmetrical design, though sometimes it is asymmetrically arranged.

The Initial Page The medieval scribe did not have a title page, but he made a splendid beginning to the book, using one or more initial letters, illuminated and gilded, followed by versals (compound capitals), in colour, written capitals and then the small text. Edward Johnston used to illustrate this arrangement by comparing the book to a regiment: the grand commander-in-chief, the officers in gay attire, the sergeants and rank and file.

The unit upon which the whole structure of the book is constructed is the interline space. (See illustrations.)

The Colophon is for the scribe's comments about how, why and when he wrote the book. The name of the calligrapher, the time and place are commonly stated, or simply a monogram and the date, nicely designed, are sufficient.

The colophon is written on a spare page at the end of the book before the end papers.

Right: Edward Johnston's 'washing-line' concept as drawn by him in my notebook. He used this analogy to illustrate the importance attached to the first writing line, showing that whilst the head margins remain constant throughout a manuscript book, the shape and length of the text columns may vary.

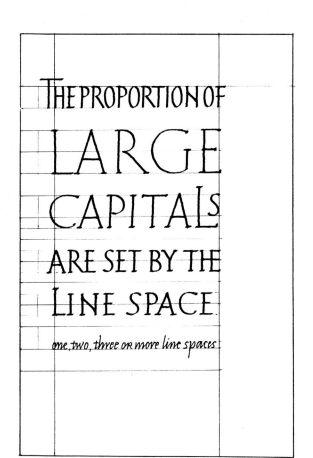

THE PROPORTION OF
LARGE
CAPITALS
ARE SET BY THE
LINE SPACE

one, two, three or more line spaces

A simple
Contrast
of weight
& colour

makes an effective
opening to a manu-
script Book

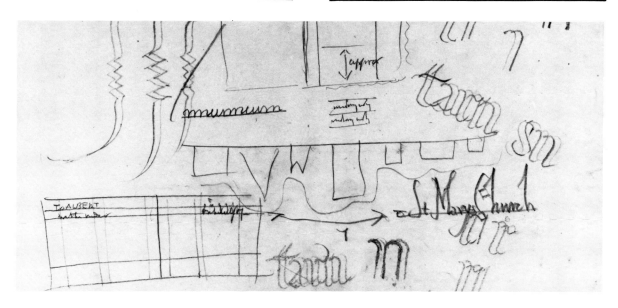

Weight
Number of nib-widths

angle
Straight pen or Slanted pen

shape
Circular, oval, flat-sided or pointed

AB	Pen-written Roman Capitals or Square Capitals.	X	OIGE	Slanted pen. 'O' Circular
ΛB	Uncials or Majuscules (large letters) Rounded forms easily and quickly written.	X	OI EFG	Straight or nearly straight. 'O' Circular
abc	Half-uncials are mixed uncials & cursive letters, our small alphabet evolved from the semi-uncial.	+	O IRISH	Straight pen 'O' Oval
abc	A Formal Roman lower-case (minuscule) alphabet which E. Johnston adapted from a 10th. century Winchester M.S.	X	oi aefg	Slanted pen. 'O' Circular
abcd	A Gothic Lower-case alphabet freely written. The letters are laterally compressed & elongated.	X	oi gothic	Slanted pen. 'O' Fractured & Flat sided & compressed
abcd	A cursive Gothic Han	X	oi cursive	Slanted pen 'O' Pointed
abcdef	A Formal Italic Hand based on a 16th. century Italian manuscript hand.	X	oi italic	Slanted pen 'O' Eliptical

Number, Order, & Direction of Strokes, and speed

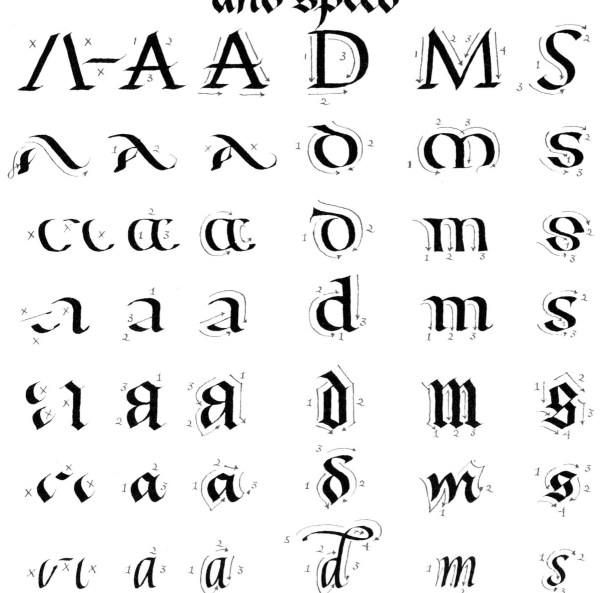

The construction of the serifs in these alphabets has not been indicated on this chart .

AN EXAMPLE OF A COMMISSIONED BOOK

When a scribe is commissioned to write a manuscript book it is essential to have in mind a general plan of the work. I am therefore including a few brief notes of my method when I wrote the St Felix School MS book.

The commission was to produce a book recording memorial gifts made to the school since its inception. It was to be kept in a specially glazed case in the school chapel, which was light and bright. It was to be written on handmade paper. I favoured an oblong-shaped book, with dimensions as follows: page size – 12 × 9 inches, top margin – 1½ inches, foot margin – 2¾ inches, inner margin – 1½ inches, outer margin – 2 inches. I suggested that it should be written in an italic hand, the general text in black, with capitals and numerals in Indian red mixed with a little white.

I made a miniature book to scale, the number of pages and sections (in this book, three) indicating on my mock-up which pages were to have single columns of long lines of writing or two columns of shorter lines of writing to a page. This is how I planned the pages:

page	
1–3	End papers
4	Calligraphic map of St Felix School and grounds (this fitted into my oblong-shaped pages very well)
5	Title page with school crest – dull green, gold and red
6	Blank
7, 8	Index – arranged in two columns
9, 10, 11, 12	The Gardiner Memorial Hall – heading in uncial capitals and small uncials in Indian red; text in black
13, 14, 15	The School Chapel – long lines of italic
16, 17, 18, 19	The Cloisters – long lines of italic
20, 21, 22	The Library – double columns
23, 24, 25, 26, 27	The Grounds – double columns
28, 29, 30, 31, 32	Miss Silcox – long lines of italic
33	Book given by two Felicians
34	Blank
35	Colophon
36–40	End papers

THIS BOOK RECORDS MEMORIAL GIFTS
MADE TO THE SCHOOL SINCE ITS INCEPTION

'The school grew from the devoted enterprise and generosity of its Foundress, her friends
who became the Governing body, colleagues on the Staff, and their successors'

Page 22 The Sunk Garden, commemorating
Old Felicians who died in the First
World War.
Miss Colman's Reading Place, com-
memorating Evelyn Ruth Colman.

23 Sheila's Garden, commemorating
Sheila Stuart Mallinson.

Flag Post, commemorating Eileen &
Elizabeth Gonner.

24 Seats, commemorating
Elizabeth Gonner.
Henry Fisher Cox
Mary Rees.

25 The Tweddle Observatory, commemorating Norman Tweddle.

Page 26 Bursary Fund, commemorating
Judith Nott.

27 Book recording Memorial Gifts,
commemorating Lucy Silcox.

THE GARDINER MEMORIAL HALL

THE HALL COMMEMORATES MARGARET ISABELLA GARDINER
(1858 – 1944), FOUNDRESS OF ST. FELIX

Miss Gardiner was the eldest daughter of Professor Samuel Rawson
Gardiner, the historian, by his wife Isabella Irving, daughter of Edward
Irving, the famous preacher. Miss Gardiner's paternal grandmother
was a member of the Baring family from whom she probably inherited her administrative ability. From her father she inherited intellectual
integrity, patience & objective judgment, & from her Irving grandfather
she derived not only her profound religious sense but her determination

9

This Book was designed & written out by
Dorothy Mahoney, Wrotham, Kent
&
bound by Sydney Cockerell, Grantchester
January 1968

Pages from the St Felix School MS book: title page, index of gifts; first page of text; colophon. (See also map, page 106.)

BINDING A SINGLE-SECTION BOOK

Given below are three simple methods of binding a single-section book.

Materials required Strong paper or thin card and a coloured or decorative paper for the outer cover; bookbinder's or buttonhole thread; scissors; a medium-sized darning needle and a strong pointed tool; pencil and ruler; tapes, coloured or plain; paper strips about 16 inches long by $\frac{1}{2}$ inch wide; plain or coloured paper or vellum strips of the same length and width.

Method 1 Cut the cover out of strong paper or thin card, making it $\frac{1}{8}$ inch larger (on all sides) than the full double-page spread. This extra allowance, commonly known as the 'square', is to protect the top, foredge and foot of the manuscript from damage.

Check that the pagination is correct and that the heads of the pages are exactly aligned, then divide the centre fold of the section into two halves and further divide the upper and lower halves into three equal parts ready for sewing. The cover paper should be showing $\frac{1}{8}$ inch all round.

Prick very carefully through the exact stitch holes with a strong pointed tool, thread the needle with thread twice the length of the book, then begin stitching from the inside out, following the diagrams carefully. To finish, tie a knot over the thread in the centre of the book, cut off the two ends of the thread about an inch from the knot.

A decorative paper could complete the book. Wrap it round the book when it is closed because the width of the spine takes up extra paper. Allow $1\frac{1}{2}$ inches for the turn-in all round – head, foredge and foot – mitre the corners and stick the turn-in down.

Method 2 Another simple method is to make a paper jacket. Sew the book as for method 1. Cut the decorative paper the height of the cover but overlapping the left and right foredges by 3 inches, turn in.

Method 3 By this method a single section is laced by tapes or paper strips. This can look effective if you use a plain dark background with light lacing, or the reverse.

Cover the stiff outer cover with plain coloured paper as for method 1 binding. Plan the lacing – long, medium and short lacings can make an attractive pattern on the cover; keep a distance of $\frac{1}{2}$ inch between the lacing in and out of the outer cover. Leave a $\frac{1}{2}$ inch from the spine before lacing the strips into the cover.

Mark the centre section ready for sewing, but remember to include the $\frac{1}{2}$-inch stitches for each of the strips. Stitch only through the book section; the lacing links the book to the cover. Folding the lacing strips into two equal parts will make both sewing and lacing simpler.

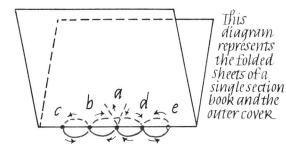

This diagram represents the folded sheets of a single section book and the outer cover

The method of stitching with a strong needle & thread a single section book.

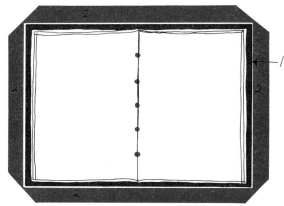

1 Stiff outer cover ⅛ inch larger than book
2 Coloured paper 3 inches wider than outer cover all round.

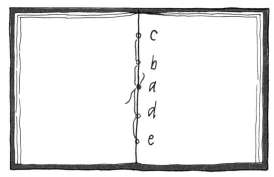

Pass the threaded needle from the centre of the book at *a* through to the back cover, leaving a length of thread inside; insert needle into the book at *b*, out again to the cover at *c*, back once more at *b*, and across to *d* & through to the back at *d*, into the centre at *e*, out once more at *d* & in at *a*. Check that the tension of the stitches is correct, tie the two ends with a knot over the long thread & cut off the thread about half an inch above knot.

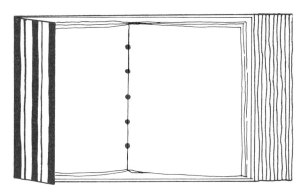

3 Bound as book above but with a decorative outer jacket overlapping the left and right foredge by 3 or 4 inches.

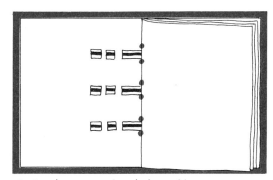

4 A single section book laced by tapes or paper strips to the cover of the book.

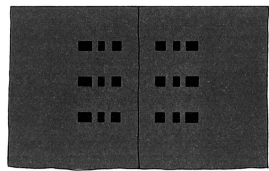

The back of a single section book laced by tapes or paper strips.

After sewing, mark the exact position of the lacing on the inside cover, draw two parallel lines across from the spine to the foredge for each lacing; mark the lacing slits and with a very sharp knife, cut the $\frac{1}{2}$-inch slits for the lacing, lace the strips into the cover. The end papers can be left free or attached to the cover.

Facing page: DAVID JONES A decorative panel of freely written Roman capitals in varying colours. David Jones was a painter, wood-engraver and letterer. He studied with Eric Gill. Jones' painted or stencilled lettering panels have influenced many contemporary scribes. Typical of his lettered panels are his mixed Greek and Roman uncials and his personal Roman capitals. He favoured soft, subtle colours – yellow ochre, sienna, yellow-green, purple, pinky mauve, soft blue-green – blending one colour into another.

ADDITIONAL ALPHABETS

SQUARE CAPITALS

These were pen-made Roman capitals. They display great dignity of form and were used from the second to the fifth century for the most important books.

RUSTIC CAPITALS

A contemporary book hand, freer, compressed and quickly written. The vertical strokes are very thin which suggests that a pen or reed was held at a very steep angle. This script was first seen in a papist's manuscript of the first century, and it survived until the beginning of the sixth century. It was commonly used as a book hand for everyday use.

ROMAN UNCIALS

The early Christian book script, which had evolved by the fourth century and remained the literary hand for fine books from the fifth to the eighth century. Roman uncials are often referred to as the 'penman's capitals'. They owe their form to the quill and to vellum, a perfect writing surface; simple strokes and rounded shapes replace the angular forms of the Roman square capitals.

ROMAN HALF-UNCIALS

These were mixed uncial and cursive letters adopted by scribes for ease and speed in writing. This script marks the beginning of the change from capitals to small letters, or minuscules. Small letters, as we know them,

ET OSTENDIT MIHI FLVVIVM AQVAE VITAE, SPLENDIDVM TAMQVAM CRYSTALLVM, PROCEDENTEM DE SEDE DEI ET AGNI. IN MEDIO PLATEAE EIVS, ET EX VTRAQVE PARTE FLVMINIS LIGNVM VITAE AFFERENS FRVCTVS DVODECIM, PER MENSES SINGVLOS REDDENS FRVCTVM SVVM, ET FOLIA LIGNI AD SANITATEM GENTIVM·

Above: EDWARD JOHNSTON Square capitals, based on those of the 3rd or 4th century. From Johnston's *A Book of Sample Scripts.*

EXTENSIS MANIBVS PROSEQVITVR QVÆ ACCEPTA HABERE DIGNERIS SICVTI QVOD TIBI OBTVLIT SVMMVS SACERDOS TVVS + MEΛXIΣEΔEK MVNERA OF LIBER ET NAIADES: POURED OUT OF CERES: BROKEN IN ANAMNHΣIΣ OF HIM WHO FREED THE WATERS ET QVI MAXIMA QVÆ QVE SACRAMENTA IN AQVARVM SVBSTANTIA CONDIDISTI

ABCDEFGHJ
KLMNOPQR
STUVWXYZ
abcdefghijklmn
opqrstuvwxyz

POSTREMO PENSANDUM,
QUANTA DOCTRINAE COMMODITAS SIT
IN LIBRIS,
QUAM FACILIS, QUAM ARCANA.
QUAM TUTO LIBRIS HUMANAE IGNORANTIAE
PAUPERTATEM SINE VERECUNDIA DENUDAMUS!
HI SUNT MAGISTRI QUI NOS INSTRUUNT
SINE VIRGIS ET FERULA, SINE VERBIS ET CHOLERA,
SINE PANNIS ET PECUNIA · SI ACCEDIS, NONDORMIUNT;
SI INQUIRENS INTERROGAS, NON ABSCONDUNT;
NON REMURMURANT, SI OBERRES;
CACHINNOS NESCIUNT, SI IGNORES ·

RICHARD DE BURY · PHILOBIBLON I. 9

SANTA BARBARA MUSEUM OF ART

DONALD JACKSON Design for a lecture announcement.

Left: JOHN WOODCOCK *Top:* Roman capitals and small letters engraved on wood. *Bottom:* A pen-written broadside written on vellum in black and red, for Philip Hofer, Houghton Library, Harvard.

fall between four imaginary horizontal lines, instead of two, as the capitals do, because of the extensions of certain letters; e.g. b, d, f, h, k and l, which have 'ascenders' and g, j, p, q and y, which have 'descenders'.

IRISH HALF-UNCIALS

These were founded on Roman half-uncials, brought to Ireland by Roman missionaries in the sixth century. The *Book of Kells*, written during the seventh century, is the most superb manuscript written in this beautiful script.

ENGLISH HALF-UNCIALS

These were modelled on Irish half-uncials. The *Lindisfarne Gospels* or the *Durham Book*, *circa* AD 700, written at Lindisfarne (Holy Island) is very like the *Book of Kells*, but is not so richly decorated and the writing is slightly heavier and wider in proportion. It is one of the most magnificent English manuscripts.

NOMINA PRAEPOSITORUM COLLEGII REGALIS

WILLIAM MILLINGTON		1441
JOHN CHEDWORTH		1447
ROBERT WODELARKE		1452
WALTER FIELD		1479
JOHN DOGGET		1499
JOHN ARGENTINE	✦	1501
RICHARD HATTON		1508
ROBERT HACUMBLEN	✦	1509
EDWARD FOX		1528
GEORGE DAY		1538
SIR JOHN CHEKE		1549
RICHARD ATKINSON		1553
ROBERT BRASSIE	✦	1556
PHILIP BAKER		1558
ROGER GOADE	✦	1570
FOGGE NEWTON		1610
WILLIAM SMITH		1612
SAMUEL COLLINS		1615
BENJAMIN WHICHCOTE		1645
JAMES FLEETWOOD		1660
SIR THOMAS PAGE	✦	1676
JOHN COPLESTONE	✦	1681
CHARLES RODERICK	✦	1689
JOHN ADAMS		1712
ANDREW SNAPE		1720
WILLIAM GEORGE	✦	1743
JOHN SUMNER	✦	1756
WILLIAM COOKE		1772
HUMPHRY SUMNER	✦	1797
GEORGE THACKERAY	✦	1814
RICHARD OKES	✦	1850
AUGUSTUS AUSTEN LEIGH		1889
MONTAGUE RHODES JAMES		1905
SIR WALTER DURNFORD		1918
ALAN ENGLAND BROOKE		1926
SIR JOHN TRESSIDDER SHEPPARD		1933
STEPHEN RANULPH KINGDON GLANVILLE		1954

BURIED IN THE CHAPEL ✦

DOROTHY MAHONEY Panel of Provosts and Fellows buried in the Chapel at King's College, Cambridge.

ABCDEFGHIIK
LMNOPQRST
UVUIXY
UNCIALS AND
half uncials. abcdefgh
ijklmnopqrstuvwxyz
Pater noster, qui est
in coelis : sanctificetur
nomen tuum.

THE QUICK BROWN
FOX JUMPS OVER
THE LAZY DOG, BASED
ON SIMPLE UNCIALS
OF THE 4TH CENTURY

FOR
UNTO US
A CHILD
IS BORN,
UNTO US
A SON
IS GIVEN:
AND HE
SHALL BE
CALLED
THE PRINCE
OF PEACE

You are invited to an
EVENING OF CHAMBER MUSIC

Bernardo Parronchi : violoncello
George Yastremsky : violin,   Jere Stern : viola
Peter Waters : pianoforte

SATURDAY, NOVEMBER 26, 1977 AT EIGHT O'clock
in the Party Room of the Promenade
5225 Pooks Hill Road, Bethesda, Maryland, FLOOR A LEVEL
Reception afterwards · Black tie optional

R·S·V·P Mrs Bernardo Parronchi, The Promenade, # 827 South Wing, 5225 Pooks Hill Rd. Bethesda, Md. 20014

Top left : A psalter from the State Archives, Namur, Belgium. The script bears a slight resemblance to certain Northumbrian characters *circa* AD 740–9.

Top right and above right : SHEILA WATERS Specimen lettering sheet based on simple uncials of the 4th century ; and invitation card written in uncial and half-uncial characters.

Above left : JOHN PRESTIANNI Design for a Christmas card (1978). Writing based on 8th-century uncial. Original size : 10 × 6½ ins (255 × 165 mm).

Alcuin's Bible. Caroline-minuscule, 9th century. (Add. MS 10546, f.262b. Wisdom i.1–6.)

CAROLINE-MINUSCULE

These are named after Charlemagne and sometimes called Carolingian. They are derived from the Continental hands which were strongly influenced by the rough Roman cursive, an undistinguished script until the end of the eighth century.

'The period of Charlemagne is an epoch in the history of handwritings of Western Europe. With the revival of learning naturally came a reform of the writing in which the works of literature were to be made known. A decree of the year 789 called for the revision of church books; and this work naturally brought with it a great activity in the writing schools of the chief monastic centres of France. And in none was there greater activity than at Tours, where, under the rule of Alcuin of York, who was abbot of St Martin's from 796 to 804, was specially developed the exact hand which has received the name of the Caroline Minuscule.' From *An Introduction to Greek and Latin Palaeography* by Sir Edward Maunde Thompson, published by Oxford University Press, 1912.

The Caroline hands spread throughout Europe, and our modern copy-books may be regarded as direct, degenerate descendants. English variants were written in southern England in the tenth century, and one, the *Winchester Psalter* (British Museum, Harley MS 2904), was the model script upon which Edward Johnston based his Foundational Hand. He described it as *'an extremely good, formal, "slanted pen" writing, having great freedom (note the very slight slope forward) and simplicity.'*

ilexifti maliciam super benignitatem · iniquitatem magifquam loqui aequitatem

ilexifti omnia uerba precipitationif· inlingua dolofa

roptcrea destru&te df infinem · euell&te &emi gmbrcte decabernaculo tuo · &radicem tuam de tcrra uiuentium

idebunt iusti &cimebunt· &supeum ridebunt &dicent·

cce homo qui non posuit dm adiutorē sedsperauit inmultitudine diuiarum suarum &preualuit inuanitate sua

go autem sicut oliua fructifera indomo dm speraui inmisericordia dei mei incternum &inseculum saeculi

onficebor tibi dne insclm quia fecisti &expecstabo nomen tuum qm bonum est· ante conspectum scorū tuorū·

QUIPOTENS ES IN iniquitate ;

ota die iniusticiam cogitauit lingua tua sicut nouacula acuta fecisti dolum

INFINEM PRO IXIT INSIPIENS incorde suo nonest df· corrupti sunt &abbo

AMALEH INTELLE mnabilef facti sunt in uoluntatibus suis ; onest qui faciat bonum·

GENTIAE DAUID· LII nonest usq: adunum ; nf decelo prospexit sup filiof hominū· ut uideat

English psalter, AD 1000. Winchester. (Harley MS 603, f.29.)

The quick brown
fox jumps over
the lazy dog.
Carolingian, 9 cent.

SHEILA WATERS Specimen lettering sheet based on Carolingian script of the 9th century.

istos psalmos cc
ego indignus de
pio in honore n
domine beate n
nis et omnium

VERNON SHEARER Small Roman letters from the scribe's notebook.

A man should forbear boastmaking
until his fierce mind fully knows
which way his spleen shall expend itself.

ANN CAMP Three lines of text of 'The Wanderer', an Anglo-Saxon poem. Initial in crimson, text in black.

Right: EDWARD JOHNSTON Foundational hand. From Johnston's *A Book of Sample Scripts.*

the earth; that all the earth may know that there is a God in Israel: and that all this assembly may know that the Lord saveth not with sword and spear: for the battle is the LORD'S, and he will give you into our hand. And it came to pass, when the Philistine a-rose, and came and drew nigh to meet David, that David hastened, and ran toward the ar-my to meet the Philistine. And David put his hand in his bag, and took thence a stone, and slang it, and smote the Philistine in his forehead; and the stone sank into his forehead, and he fell upon his face to the earth. So David prevailed over the Philis-tine with a sling and with a stone, and smote the Philistine, and slew him; but there was

10th-, 11th- AND 12th-CENTURY WRITING

The use of the slanted pen and consequent lateral compression resulted in valuable economy of time and space in writing manuscript books. In the eleventh and twelfth centuries it caused curves to give place to angles, and writing became 'Gothic' in character.

Early 15th-century manuscript of Thomas Hoccleve's *De Regimine Principum* with a portrait of Geoffrey Chaucer (d. 1400). It was painted, as Hoccleve says, *to putte othir men in remembrance of his persone.*

13th-, 14th- AND 15th-CENTURY WRITING

Compression continued, and in the thirteenth and fourteenth centuries further economy of space took place through the general use of much smaller writing. In the fifteenth century writing again grew larger and taller, letters became narrower and more angular. The written page consisted of rows of perpendicular thick strokes with heads and feet connected by oblique hair-lines, which often look as if they had been dashed in later with a fine pen.

Inset, facing page: Passage from a late 15th-century manuscript of Froissart. (British Museum, Harley MS 4379.)

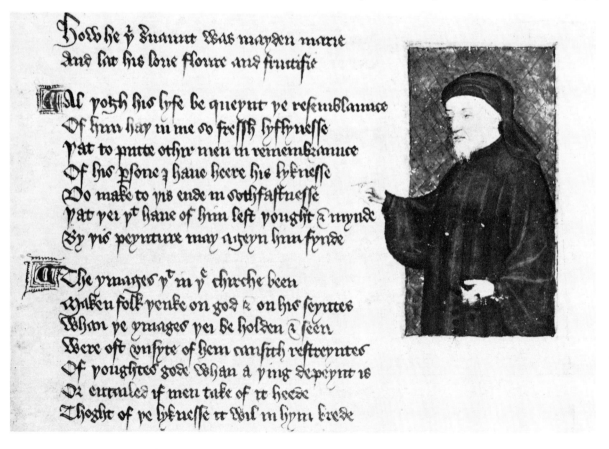

Black Letter

ABCDEF
GHJKLM
NOPQRS
TUVWX
YZ

abcdefghijkl
mnopqrstu
vwxyz

Cursive Gothic

abcdefghijkl
mnopqrstu
wxyz

aincontre et auone nous parle
trop continuement et retourne
vne auv bawne et cheualiere
de france qui aincontre tenoi
ent le siege deuant la forte
et puissant ville dauffricque
la ou ilz eurent de moult gra
des escarmouches que lee sar
rasins leur faisoient continu
ellement dont y morurent
maint homme tant noble cõ
non noble dequoy ce fut maint
dommaige.

¶Comment et par quelle Inca
dense le siege fut leue de de
uant la forte ville dauffric
que: Et comment chascun sen
retourna en son lieu.

Lines from the first Book of The Bruce.

A ffredome is A noble ying,
ffredome mayse man to hauff liking,
ffredome all solace to man giffis,
He leuys at ese yat frely leuys,
A noble hart may hauff nane ese,
Na ellys nocht yat may him plese,
Gyff fredome failzhe for fre liking,
Is zharnyt our all oyir ying,
Na he yat ay hase leuyt fre,
May nocht knaw Weill ye propyrte,
Ye angyr na ye Wretchyt Dome,
Yat is cowplyt to foule yyrldome,
Bot gyff he had assayit It,
Fan all perquer he suld It Wyt,
And suld yink fredome mar to pryse,
Fan all ye gold in Warld yat Is,
Sus contrar yingis euir mar,
Discoweryngis off ye toyir ar,

EDWARD JOHNSTON Lines from the first *Book of the Bruce* by John Barbour, *circa* 1320–95. Written in a contemporary hand with text in black and notes in red.

RUDOLF KOCH *Above:* Typical pen-written Gothic alphabet. *Below:* Lombardic Gothic, with fat, curvacious capitals and lower-case letters. (From *The Little ABC Book of Rudolf Koch*, published by The Merrion Press, London, 1976.)

FORMAL AND SEMI-FORMAL ITALIC

During the early period of the Italian Re-naissance Florentine scholars discovered classical manuscripts written in the Caroline-minuscule during the ninth century, and these they copied and adapted for their own use. One adaptation became the origin of our small roman type, the other became the formal italic which flourished during the fifteenth and sixteenth centuries in Italy and in Spain.

The form of the italic hand is essentially the result of speed and rhythm of the writing which is much quicker than that of the formal roman minuscule. Speed caused lateral com-pression and branching, an elliptical O, twice as high as it is wide, became the key letter for curved forms. This, together with the nar-rowing of the broad nib, gave the script a natural lightness of weight which was echoed in the lengthening of ascenders and de-scenders often extravagantly flourished. A tendency to move quickly to the right led to the arched letters branching away from the stem. This produced a slight slope to the right and was particularly noticeable in the letters *b*, *p*, *h*, *m* and *n* (clockwise movement) and *a*, *d*, *g*, *u* and *y* (counter-clockwise movement); *a*, like *d*, *b*, *p*, *g* and *q*, was constructed from the same elliptical O form.

A simple serif was made by pushing the pen upwards before beginning the down stroke, or alternately the top of the ascender might be hooked, or curved to the right.

Inter-line spacing was generally very open, but italics can be tightly packed when ascenders and descenders would be shortened, possibly for marginal notes and so on.

Italic capitals were slightly compressed Roman capitals, or sometimes Roman cap-itals written small. They may be upright or sloping slightly. Flourished capitals are fun to write but should be used with discretion.

Formal Italic

o abcdefghijk

abcdefghijklm

Characteristics of the Formal Italic Hand.

lmnopqrstuv

Lateral compression and Branching.

nopqrstuvwxy

Perpendicular movement & Flourishing.

wxyz & ambn

The Italic 'o' is based on an oval

z n u r

vi abdg c c e

(i) o p p q q

h h m m n u

f f k k l

r s l t

v v w x y z

& ct st sp g v

ABCDEFGHIJ
KLMNOPQRS
TUVWXYZ

Slightly compressed Roman Capitals, the
curved letters are based on an eliptical 'O'.

ABCDE&F
GHIJKLM
NOPQRST
UVWXYZ

Flourished Capitals that may be used
with lower-case Italic.

A B C D E

Some varieties of Round Flourished Capitals.

E F G H IJ

Capitals with exaggerated serifs, heads,

K L M N O
P Q R S T U
U W X Y Z

arms, tails and bodies.

Characteristics of the Italic Hand

1 Lateral compression &

2 Branching

3 Perpendicular movement &

4 Flourishing.

The Italic alphabet developed from quickly written, laterally compressed Roman Capitals and small letters. The circular 'o' was squeezed to an oval, approx twice as high as it was wide; all curved Italic letters are based on an oval.

o n u r a d u g b p h m n c e

Branching to the right gives a slight slope to Italic writing: elongation of ascenders and descenders and restrained flourishes gives a charm & elegance to this alphabet, which is much used by Calligraphers today.

The quick brown fox jumps over the Lazy dog.

Italic or Semi-formal writing

The cursive, or running hand, as Edward Johnston called it, is based on the same forms as the Italic hand but it is written at a greater speed; the pen travels as far as it can without a pen lift.

The letters are linked by thin diagonal ligatures which spring from the base of a c d h i k l m n t u

The basic rhythms run in a clockwise and counter-clockwise direction. mmm uuuu

ambmcmdmemfmgmhmin jukulumunupupuourusutu vuwuxuyuzu abcdefghyklmnopqrst uv& wxy z

ROMA
NORVM
Olympias. cclxxv.

XIIII.

XV.

XVI.

XVII.   Constantinus Constantini filius Cæsar factus.
Olympias. cclxxvi.
                                           A sacramenti
XVIII. Lycinius Thessalonicæ contra uis sacra priuatus occiditur.
XIX.   Nazarius Rhætor insignis habetur.
XX.   Crispus filius Constantini & Lycinius iunior Constantiæ Constan-
        tini sororis & Lycinij superioris filius crudelissime interficiun-
        tur anno imperij sui .ix.
        Vicenalia Constantini Nicomediæ acta .& sequenti anno Romæ edita.

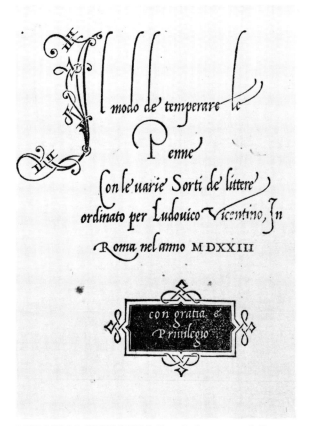

LUDOVICO VICENTINO *Il modo de temperare le Penne.* Rome, 1523.

Left: BARTOLOMEO SANVITO *Eusebius* written for Bernardo Bembo (British Museum, Chronica. Royal 14. C.3). The following quote about Sanvito, who was born in Padua in 1435, is taken from *The Script of Humanism* by James Wardrop, published by Oxford University Press, 1963: *No one could set out a page of capitals as he did; and he wrote them in characteristic fashion: alternate lines of gold, blue, lake, purple, violet and green. He who can write Roman capitals can write anything, said Gianfrancesco Cresci almost a century later.*

LUDOVICO VICENTINO A page from *Regola da imparare scrivere.*

Right: EDWARD JOHNSTON A page of italics from my Johnston notebook.

Below: DOROTHY MAHONEY Memorial panel in St Mary's Church, Platt, written for Mrs Joscelyne Charlewood Turner. On vellum in black ink with burnished gold initial and notes in blue. Framed.

Facing page: WILLIAM GARDNER The third 'Amoretti' sonnet composed by Edmund Spenser, 1595.

If a man's being is rooted in one steadfast piece of earth which has nourished him and if he can on his side lend it glory & do it service it will be a friend to him forever. and he has outflanked death in a way.

Reflection by Rupert Brooke

CHARLES AUSTIN CHARLEWOOD TURNER A.R.I.B.A. 1892 ~ 1967
Captain, late The Connaught Rangers
CHURCH WARDEN 1930 ~ 1966

The third "AMORETTI" sonnet

What guile is this, that those her golden tresses
She doth attire under a net of gold;
And with sly skill so cunningly them dresses,
That which is gold or hair, may scarce be told?
Is it that men's frail eyes, which gaze too bold,
She may entangle in that golden snare;
And being caught may craftily enfold
Their weaker hearts, which are not well aware?
Take heed therefore, mine eyes, how ye do stare
Henceforth too rashly on that guileful net,
In which if ever ye entrapped are,
Out of her bands ye by no means shall get.
Fondness it were for any being free,
To covet fetters, though they golden be.

Composed by Edmund Spenser, 1595.

DONALD JACKSON Flourished italics in red and black.

di Signor le preghiere mie ogni uolta chio
chiamo il nome tuo; habbi misericordia
me; & non sperzar le uoie di chi con hui-
milta ti chiama.

VERNON SHEARER Freely copied italics.

In
Romney
Marsh

John
Davidson
12

As I went down to Dymchurch wall,
 I heard the South sing o'er the land;
I saw the yellow sunlight fall
 On knolls where Norman churches stand.

And ringing shrilly, taut and lithe,
 Within the wind a core of sound,
The wire from Romney town to Hythe
 Along its airy journey wound.

A veil of purple vapour flowed
 And trailed its fringe along the Straits;
The upper air like sapphire glowed;
 And roses filled Heaven's central gates.

Masts in the offing wagged their tops;
 The swinging waves pealed on the shore;
The saffron beach, all diamond drops
 And beads of surge, prolonged the roar.

As I came up from Dymchurch wall,
 I saw above the Downs' low crest
The crimson brands of sunset fall,
 Flicker and fade from out the west.

Night sank: like flakes of silver fire
 The stars in one great shower came down;
Shrill blew the wind; and shrill the wire
 Rang out from Hythe to Romney town.

The darkly shining salt sea drops
 Streamed as the waves clashed on the shore;
The beach, with all its organ stops
 Pealing again, prolonged the roar.

JOAN PILSBURY 'In Romney Marsh' by John Davidson. Double-page opening in vellum. Text in black with gold initials. Bound in paper by the scribe.

Society of Scribes & Illuminators

IEUAN REES Logo for the Society of Scribes and Illuminators.

THE GREEKS HAD A WORD FOR IT
Kalligraphia,
meaning "beautiful writing."
THE CHINESE used two words for it *Shu-fa*
meaning "the system or method of writing."

HEATHER CHILD Quotation from *Chinese Calligraphy* by Tseng Yu-Ho Ecke.

·WATERSHIP DOWN·

Presented to
H.M.Ambassador to the
Federal Republic of
Germany

Sir Oliver Wright, KCMG DSC

on the occasion of his visit to the
Frankfurt Book Fair
on 20th September
1976

JOHN WOODCOCK A dedication page in a presentation copy of *Watership Down*.

VERSALS

Versals were a variety of built-up (compound) Roman capitals, used to mark important parts of the text. When small letters were used for the main body of the text, capitals became distinguishing letters for headings and important words, and these letters were picked out in colour and often decorated. They were used for the beginning of books, chapters, paragraphs, and to mark the beginning of verses; hence the word versal.

A versal letter is built up with a definite number of pen strokes, using a pen which has a long slit of $\frac{1}{2}-\frac{3}{4}$ inch to make it more flexible (see illustration). The nib width is less than that used for the text. The writing board is lowered to allow thick liquid colour to flow freely from the pen. The outlining strokes are written first and then are immediately flooded with colour.

Early versals were based on the classical Roman capital letter. They are the best models for the beginner who has a reasonable idea of the structure and relative proportion of the Roman capitals. The later Lombardic versals were frequently based on the round uncial letters. The broad-nibbed pen no longer controls the letter form, as it does in the simple written capital.

A thorough knowledge of letter design, of spacing and arrangement is essential if you wish to experiment with these intriguing letters.

Versal letters are usually in colour. Two of the most effective colours are black and vermilion red, though other colours can of course be used.

Facing page: ANN HECHLE Modern built-up versals from a Calligraphic Sampler sponsored by the Victoria and Albert Museum (London) and also by the Crafts Council, 1979.

Overleaf (page 93): 'Libellus' – freely drawn copy of titling from a Visigothic manuscript of 954 in the Escorial, Madrid (Cod. a. 11. 9. f.6v.). An extremely attenuated tall versal with decorative serifs.

'Dilectis' – copied in detail from a Bull of Pope Gregory IX of 1228. (Rome, Archivio di Stato.) A rich decorative gothic 'D', heavy in weight, acts as a foil to the extraordinary extended ascenders of the small letters.

'Erba' – richly rounded 'fruity' versals freely copied from those found in a 12th-century French manuscript.

'Divinis' – a single word copied from the incipit lines of a French bible of about 1200. The elliptical 'D' comfortably contains the 'IVINIS'.

(Copied by the author from Nicolette Gray's *Lettering as Drawing*, Oxford University Press, London, 1971.)

BUILT-UP LETTERS FLOODED IN

VERSALS

SWAGGER SIMPLE

each according to its function

decorative

alternatively in reverse

THERE IS AN ADDITIONAL

according to the flavour

PROBLEM IN THAT RED IS A

of the text. A minuscule

DIFFERENT TONE TO BLACK,

has a more cursive and a

WHICH REDUCES ITS IMPACT.

more informal character

italic branching arches

VERSAL CAPITALS

a type of built-up or compound Roman Capital used to mark important parts of the text & so they are generally in colour. VERSALS vary in form from the classical Roman Capitals to the extravagant Lombardic letters, rich in weight, shape and design but not very legible.

Use a long slit for Versal letters and lower the board so that the liquid colour flows quickly between the two strokes of the stem. The hair-line serif cuts the thick stroke at right angles.

Stems & Serifs Narrowest part of a. Stems first stem approx. three b. Serifs first nib widths.

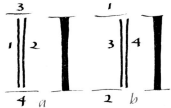

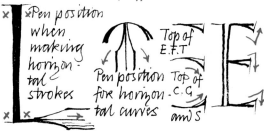

Pen position when making horizontal strokes

Pen position for horizontal curves

Top of E.F.T

Top of C.G and S

Thin serif with thick stem

Sharp right angles for VERSALS

Serifs blend into the

built up Roman Capital

O O O

Narrow flat   Normal bow   Wide curved.

ABCDE

Component parts or Pen-strokes

ABCDEF

Roman Capitals or Square Capitals

GHIJKL

MNOP

RSTUW

XYZ

ABCDE
GhiKLM
MPPQR
SCsTVw

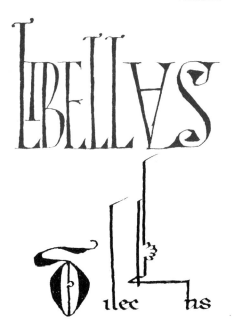

Round forms of X Versal letters

The Head of an ascending stroke
looks better if it is slightly wider
than the foot: the stem width is
the same in Versals of varying
height.

Construction of bows (a)

Flat
curve   Norm-   Flat   Curved
         al

Construction of 'Bows'. (b)

Begin Bows & Curves with a flatish inside stroke: finish the outer stroke with
a pronounced curve.

Arms or Branches the width of the nib at
start, the free end is built up into a wedge
shape. EFL CGS

A variety of decorative Versal Letters
from X, XII and XIII century M.S.S.

ILLUSTRATIONS FROM MS BOOKS

Psalter. Late 10th century. (Harley MS 2904, f.125.)

JOAN PILSBURY Page from *Record of Arms of the Prime Wardens of the Fishmongers' Company*, Volume 1. Vellum, full colour and gold. Original size: 12½ × 9½ ins (320 × 240 mm).

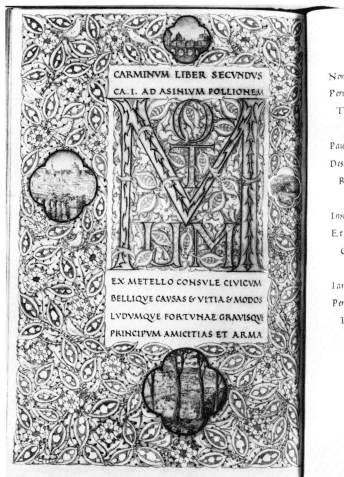

CARMINVM LIBER SECVNDVS
CA. 1. AD ASINIVM POLLIONEM

EX METELLO CONSVLE CIVICVM
BELLIQVE CAVSAS & VITIA & MODOS
LVDVMQVE FORTVNAE GRAVISQVE
PRINCIPVM AMICITIAS ET ARMA

Nondum expiatis uncta cruoribus,
Periculosae plenum opus aleae,
  Tractas, et incedis per ignis
    Suppositos cineri doloso.
Paulum severae Musa tragoediae
Desit theatris: mox ubi publicas
  Res ordinaris, grande munus
    Cecropio repetes cothurno,
Insigne maestis praesidium reis
Et consulenti, Pollio, curiae,
  Cui laurus aeternos honores
    Delmatico peperit triumpho.
Iam nunc minaci murmure cornuum
Perstringis auris, iam litui strepunt,
  Iam fulgor armorum fugaces
    Terret equos equitumque vultus

ALFRED FAIRBANK and LOUISE POWELL Horace: *Odes and Epodes.* Writing and gilding by Alfred Fairbank, illuminating by Louise Powell, 1927–1931. Original page size: 9 × 6 ins (230 × 150 mm).

WHO LIVETH ALONE
LONGETH FOR MERCY
MAKER'S MERCY
THOUGH HE MUST TRAVERSE
TRACTS OF SEA, SICK AT HEART
– TROUBLE WITH OARS
ICE COLD WATERS
THE WAYS OF EXILE –
WIERD IS SET FAST

Thus spoke such a 'crasshopper'
old criefs in his mind,
cold slauchters,
the death of dear kinsmen:

'Alone am I driven each day before daybreak
to give my cares utterance.
None are there now among the living
to whom I dare declare me throughly
tell my heart's thought. Too truly I know

ANN CAMP and ALISON URWICK 'The Wanderer', an Anglo-Saxon poem, taken from a Penguin Classic *The Earliest English Poems* (published 1966, London). Written out by Ann Camp and illustrated by Alison Urwick by permission of the translator Michael Alexander. Original size: 24 × 16¾ ins (610 × 430 mm).

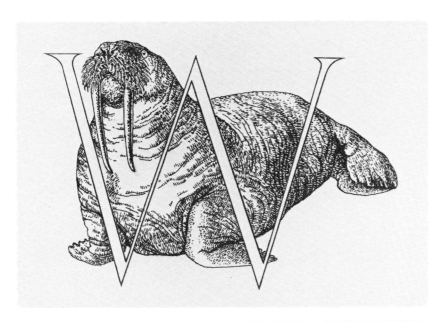

Left: MARIE ANGEL Walrus
letter in black and white from
Two By Two, an alphabet book
by Toby Talbot, published by
Follett Publishing Co, Chicago,
USA, 1974.

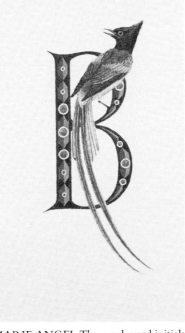

MARIE ANGEL Three coloured initials
from *Tucky, the Hunter* by James Dickey,
published by Crown Publishers, New
York, USA, 1978 and Macmillan,
London, 1979.

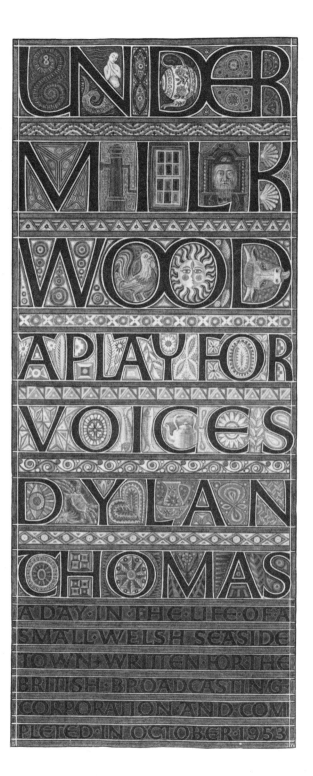

Right and facing page: SHEILA WATERS *Under Milk Wood – A Play for Voices* by Dylan Thomas. Written and illuminated by Sheila Waters and bound by her husband Peter Waters. Illustrated are the title page and page three.

coughing like nannygoats, sucking mintoes, fortywinking hallelujah; night in the four-ale, quiet as a domino; in Ocky Milkman's lofts like a mouse with gloves; in Dai Bread's bakery flying like black flour. It is tonight in Donkey Street, trotting silent, with seaweed on its hooves, along the cockled cobbles, past curtained fernpot, text and trinket, harmonium, holy dresser, watercolours done by hand, china dog and rosy tin teacaddy. It is night neddying among the snuggeries of babies.

Look. It is night, dumbly, royally winding through the Coronation cherry trees; going through the graveyard of Bethesda with winds gloved and folded, and dew doffed; tumbling by the Sailors Arms.

Time passes. Listen. Time passes.

Come closer now.

Only you can hear the houses sleeping in the streets in the slow deep salt and silent black, bandaged night. Only you can see, in the blinded bedrooms, the combs and petticoats over the chairs, the jugs and basins, the glasses of teeth, Thou Shalt Not on the wall, and the yellowing dicky-bird-watching pictures of the dead. Only you can hear and see, behind the eyes of the sleepers, the movements and countries and mazes and colours and

3

DOROTHY MAHONEY A transcription in book form of Horace Walpole's
letter from Houghton to George Montagu Esq, 25th March 1761, written out and
bound as a Christmas greeting to Lord and Lady Cholmondeley (about 1952).
Written on vellum in black stick ink with indian red headings. Bound by the
author in a Cockerell marbled paper.

BROADSHEETS OR BROADSIDES

The simplest broadsheet keeps to the proportions of the book page but as it is a single sheet it is symmetrically arranged and written or printed on one side only. The head and foot margins are in the ratio 2:4 respectively, like a book, but both side margins are the same width, namely $2\frac{1}{2}$ units wide. (See illustration.)

If a broadsheet is to be framed the margins may be smaller because the frame isolates the manuscript from its surroundings. Moreover, it is necessary to know where the broadsheet is to hang – in the home, a public hall, church, school or so on – and the source and amount of light available, as these factors will affect the impact given and produced by the size and form of the writing.

IRENE WELLINGTON The Bailiffs of Lydd, a framed panel on vellum, which hangs in the Council Chamber of the Guildhall, Lydd. The names are written in Roman minuscules, a compact letter to give weight and legibility at eye-level. The capitals in the introduction at the top are drawn with a pen. The title, in black and white capitals, is written on a wide band of matt gold. Original size: 2 ft 10 ins × 3 ft 5 ins (865 × 1040 mm).

BANCO INTERAMERICANO DE DESARROLLO

EXHIBICION

El Arte en la Artesanía de México

OCTUBRE DE 1978 — MARZO DE 1979

TESTIMONIO DE RECONOCIMIENTO AL

Sr. José Guadalupe Sánchez

Por la generosa colaboración prestada para la
presentación en la sede del Banco Interamericano
de Desarrollo en Washington, D.C., Estados Unidos
de América, de una muestra de las más selectas
expresiones del arte contemporáneo de México.

La colección, formada por un variado conjunto
de exquisitas piezas de artesanía, ofreció a los
ciudadanos y autoridades de esta capital la
oportunidad de conocer y valorar la fuerza
creativa del arte mexicano, reflejada a través de
una de las más genuinas manifestaciones
del rico acervo cultural que posee
nuestra gran Nación.

Washington, D.C.
31 de marzo de 1979

Antonio Ortiz Mena
Presidente

JULIAN WATERS An address to Sr José Guadalupe
Sánchez from the Banco Interamericano de Desarrollo.
Written in a slightly sloping formal italic. A broadsheet
with handsome margins. Original size: 17 × 11 ins
(430 × 280 mm).

Right: DOROTHY MAHONEY and MARIE ANGEL
'The Prayer of St Francis', written on vellum by Dorothy
Mahoney with initial capitals and animals painted by Marie
Angel. Title and cross in raised gold, text in black, uncial
capitals and the last four lines in blue. Original size:
9 × 22 ins (230 × 560 mm).

Facing page: ALEXANDER O'SULLIVAN A sonnet by
William Shakespeare, written on cream paper in a
compressed, pointed, upright italic; initial 'S' double-
stroked. Original size: 8¼ × 11¾ ins (210 × 300 mm). (1979)

THE PRAYER OF ST FRANCIS

LORD make me channel
of Thy peace.

THAT where there is hatred,
I may bring love;

THAT where there is wrong,
I may bring the spirit of forgiveness;

THAT where there is discord,
I may bring harmony;

THAT where there is error,
I may bring truth;

THAT where there is doubt,
I may bring faith;

THAT where there is despair,
I may bring hope;

AND where there are shadows,
I may bring Thy light;

THAT where there is sadness,
I may bring joy.

LORD grant that I may seek
rather to comfort, than be comforted.

TO understand, than be understood.
To love, than be loved;

FOR it is by giving, that one receives.
IT is by self forgetting, that one finds.
IT is by forgiving that one is forgiven.
IT is by dying that one awakens to
Eternal Life.

SONNET

NO. XVIII. BY WILLIAM SHAKESPEARE

Shall I compare thee to a summer's day?
Thou art more lovely and more temperate.
Rough winds do shake the darling buds of May,
And summer's lease hath all too short a date:
Sometime too hot the eye of heaven shines,
And often is his gold complexion dimm'd;
And every fair from fair sometime declines,
By chance, or nature's changing course, untrimm'd;
But thy eternal summer shall not fade,
Nor lose possession of that fair thou ow'st;
Nor shall Death brag thou wander'st in his shade,
When in eternal lines to time thou grow'st.
So long as men can breathe, or eyes can see,
So long lives this, and this gives life to thee.

From calligraphy by A. O'Sullivan, Member of The Craftsmen of Gloucestershire. 79

DOROTHY MAHONEY Lakeland Flower Tapestry, presented to Heather Child by members of the Society of Scribes and Illuminators in 1971. Lakeland wild flowers interwoven with 'Lines composed a few miles above Tintern Abbey' by William Wordsworth (13 July 1798). On vellum, flowers painted in watercolour. Lettering black, names of flowers in pale blue. The last line in a pinky mauve, echoing the colour of the bird's-eye primrose and the common butterwort. Original size: 18 × 13 ins (460 × 330 mm).

SHEILA DONALDSON-WALTERS 'In a Cathedral', a
poem by the scribe's son, Justin Vincent Walters. Freely
written and illustrated with the same pen. Original size:
10 × 12 ins (255 × 305 mm).

ANN HECHLE From 'March' by Edward Thomas. Stick
ink and watercolour on vellum. Raised and burnished gold
leaf; burnished gold leaf and thinned gesso. Original size:
$4\frac{1}{2}$ × 9 ins (115 × 230 mm).

EPHEMERA

To illustrate a few of the many aspects of lettering design covered by the term 'ephemera' I have selected designs for reproduction by professional calligraphers, such as, cards (Christmas cards), logos, letter-headings, decorative headings, illustrated booklets, etc.

LES MOCQUETS POISSON 71600 PARAY LE MONIAL

SHEILA DONALDSON-WALTERS Logo.

Left and below: DOROTHY MAHONEY Decorative pen-made letters and map of the grounds of St Felix School, Southwold (see also pages 60–1).

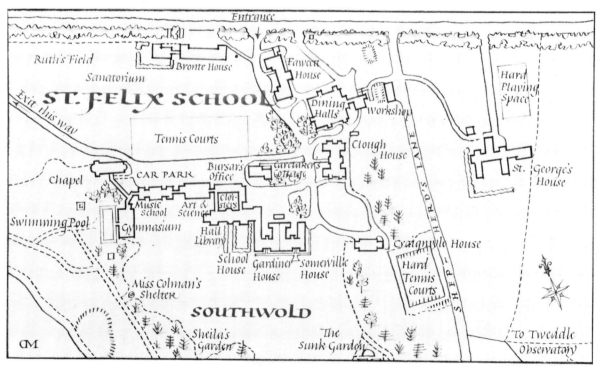

THE SOCIETY OF
SCRIBES AND
ILLUMINATORS
REQUESTS THE
HONOUR OF YOUR
ATTENDANCE
AT A LECTURE
GIVEN BY
DONALD JACKSON
ON CALLIGRAPHIC
PRACTICALITIES
ILLUSTRATED BY
SLIDES AND FILMS
ON MONDAY·
21·OCTOBER·1974·
AT·7·PM·THE CHAIR
WILL BE TAKEN
BY HEATHER CHILD
AT THE ROYAL
SOCIETY OF ARTS
JOHN ADAM ST·
ADELPHI

Calligraphic Practicalities

R·S·V·P·   Secretary to the Society John McCracken   6 Queen Square   Bloomsbury   London WCIN 3AR

DONALD JACKSON Invitation card for a lecture.

Left: DONALD JACKSON and JOHN LAWRENCE A page from Cranks' booklet. Wood engraving by John Lawrence, lettering by Donald Jackson.

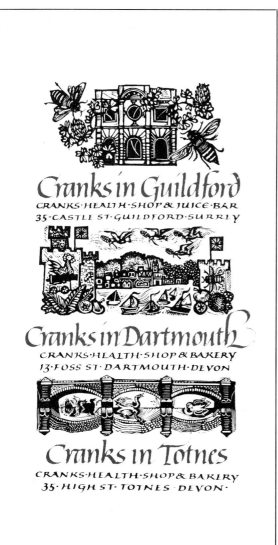

Cranks in Guildford
CRANKS·HEALTH·SHOP & JUICE·BAR
35·CASTLE ST·GUILDFORD·SURREY

Cranks in Dartmouth
CRANKS·HEALTH·SHOP & BAKERY
13·FOSS ST·DARTMOUTH·DEVON

Cranks in Totnes
CRANKS·HEALTH·SHOP & BAKERY
35·HIGH ST·TOTNES·DEVON·

Wednesday June 30		Thursday July 1	
8/9.30 am	Breakfast served in bedroom. Just fill in card and leave outside.	8/9.30 am	Breakfast served in bedroom
10.30 am	Coach to WRIGHTON Showroom, Le Cannet	10.30am	Coach leaves for panoramic trip along the Côte d'Azur, arriving
12.00 am	Informal buffet lunch, taste the local wine		at Club Figueirette approximately
1.30 pm	Coach departs for Cannes Harbour for private boat trips to islands.	11.30 am	bathing- beach pedalos. lots of fun- or relax on the terrace.
	Alternative: Swimming and sunbathing on Carlton Beach	12.30 pm	A la carte lunch at Figueirette. Relax on beach and terrace. Villa Florence
4.00 pm	Tea, coffee and sandwiches		
5.00 pm	Cocktails on board Cruise along the coast to Miramar	3.00pm	Return to Carlton, Cannes
7.00 pm	Disembark at Club Figueirette/ or by car to Club Figueirette.	4.00pm	Coach leaves for Airport.
8.30 pm	Cocktails and dine No table plan - à la carte - choose carefully and enjoy French cooking at its best.		
11.00 pm	Coach leaves for Carlton, Cannes. Arrival approximately midnight - earlier by Request		

SHEILA DONALDSON-WALTERS Pages from a Wrighton International Itinerary.

Right: JOHN WOODCOCK Bookplate in hand-drawn lettering.

Taylor Institution Library OXFORD

PRESENTED BY

DOROTHY MAHONEY Christmas cards.

MOTTE

Motif

Elephants

JOHN WOODCOCK Hand-drawn lettering designs.

Doctor
Zhivago

The Crafts Centre of Great Britain

ANN CAMP Invitation card cover.

BOOK JACKETS
AND PRINTED WORKS

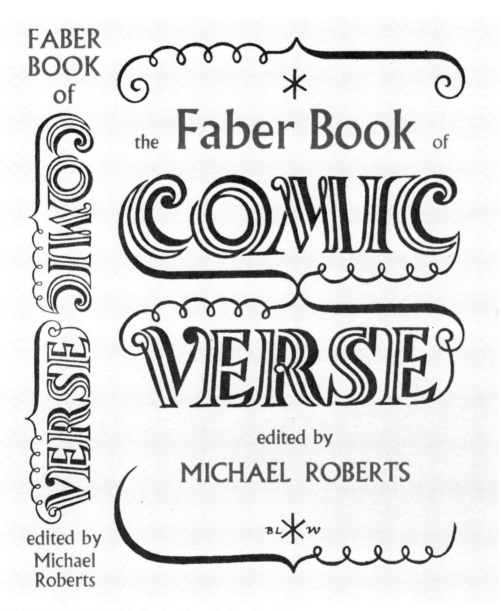

BERTHOLD WOLPE Book jacket for Faber. Black and royal blue on orange.

JOHN WOODCOCK Book jacket for Chatto and Windus. White and black on blue.

Rosemary
Haughton

Six Saints for Parents

Six
Saints
for
Parents

Rosemary
Haughton

VERNON SHEARER Book jacket for Burns & Oates. Grey and rust on cream.

MARIE ANGEL Cover design for *Two By Two*, an alphabet book by Tony Talbot, published by Follett Publishing Co, Chicago, USA, 1974.

IEUAN REES One of many sub-headings for a printed Welsh Bible. Colour: vermilion.

FRITZ KREDEL Nautical illustration taken from the cover design for a children's ABC, published by the Merrion Press, London, 1976.

HANDWRITING

The study of formal book hands should lead to an interest in informal, everyday handwriting. Here the essential qualities are speed and legibility, and economy of all unnecessary strokes.

The cursive or running hand is a no-time-to-spare handwriting, when the pen travels as far as it can without a pen lift. Compression and branching of the letter forms are similar to the formal italic hand and there is a slight slope to the right. Some letters are linked by a thin diagonal ligature which springs from the base of one letter to the top of the next, other letters are linked by horizontal ligatures. Capitals are kept small; classical Roman capitals or italic capitals based on an elliptical O are most commonly used. Spacing and arrangement are as important as for formal writing but can be lightheartedly used, which adds to the fun when writing letters to friends.

I have selected examples of handwriting for this book which I think will be of interest.

WILLIAM GARDNER Calligrapher, designer of coins and heraldic specialist.

The Scribe

What lovely things
Thy hand hath made.
The smooth-plumed bird
In its emerald shade,
The seed of the grass
The speck of stone
Which the wayfaring ant
Stirs — and hastes on

Though I should sit
By some tarn in thy hills
Using its ink
As the spirit wills
To write of Earth's wonders
Its live willed things
Flit would the ages
On soundless wings
Ere unto Z
My pen drew nigh;
Leviathan told
And the honey-fly:
And still would remain
My wit to try —
My worn reeds broken,
The dark tarn dry,
All words forgotten —
Thou, Lord, and I.

Walter de la Mare
April 1925

WALTER DE LA MARE Poet and novelist.

The Fallow Deer
at the Lonely House

One without looks in to-night
    Through the curtain-chink
From the sheet of glistening white:
One without looks in to-night
    As we sit & think
    By the fender-brink.

We do not discern those eyes
    Watching in the snow;
Lit by lamps of rosy dyes
We do not discern those eyes
    Wondering, aglow,
    Fourfooted, tiptoe.

March 1925.   Thomas Hardy.

(For Cheltenham College Library.)

THOMAS HARDY Novelist and poet.

16 October 1980

Dear Bish,

I am so pleased to hear that your book on calligraphy is to be published in the New Year. You were the one who started me off on this business of beautiful writing but when I see your hand or John Woodcock's, or our dear old Louis Prince's hand I despair. It is, I think, so much a matter of the type of pen, paper, angle of writing surface and after all these years the right type eludes me. Time in which to write and make beautiful marks is also important and there seems to be less and less of it as the years go by. I'm making time for this missive so perhaps it is worth $\frac{5}{10}$ and not too bad a sample of my hand. Let me have a tiny piece of your writing when you have finished getting your book together - please. -
Keep well, affectionately
Gordon Ransom

GORDON RANSOM Painter and Head of Graphic Design at St Martins School of Art, London.

SILVER LEY,

OAKLEY ROAD,

WARLINGHAM, SURREY,

Telephone: Upper Warlingham 4380

Above and right: MARIE ANGEL Illustrator and calligrapher.

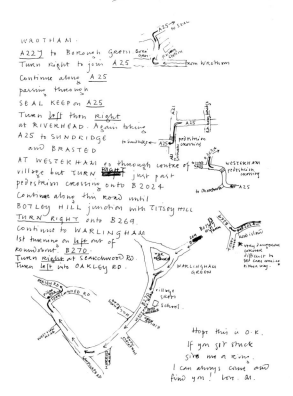

Dear Dorothy,

Many thanks for yr. reminder! I am afraid I have become lazy in writing & scribble instead! Irene in remarking on that, excused me on the ground that the press of every day existence didn't allow enough time for such relaxed luxuries as writing.

You manage it, even with a ball point but it's your job! When Alfred asked me for what you are now asking, I made a horrible mess with unsuitable pen & ink on paper (handmade) which didn't really give me a chance, & I am now surprised that he used it. You might well do best to make use of something you have already?

I once put together a collection of letters for Sir Sydney & was told to include one from me to him, written about the project. I imagine I tried not to disgrace myself in writing any letter to him. That is what I am trying to do now, for you!

All well & rather seriously overloaded with work.

love Roger. 17/VI/1980

ROGER POWELL Designer bookbinder who with Peter Waters rebound the *Book of Kells*.

Douglas Cockerell & Son   Dec 1st 1969

Bookbinders and makers of marbled paper   Riversdale Grantchester Cambridge   Trumpington (OCA 021) 2124

Dear Dorothy,

Thank you for your letter enclosing your drawing for the R.E. blocks
A great improvement!
I am having a reversed photostat made as I cannot quite visualise your block as fatd.
By all means send your "Rustic Adornments" for first aid.

Sandy

SYDNEY COCKERELL Designer bookbinder.

W·R·Lethaby

WILLIAM LETHABY Distinguished architect and friend of William Morris.

7 Lansdown Place East, Bath
1 Nov. 1949

Dear Mrs. Mahoney

I am glad to accept the kind invitation to lecture to R.C.A. students early next year. Friday afternoon might be the better time, but I think I cd. equally well come on a Thursday evening. Really I leave that to you.

I shd. enjoy talking about italics & wd. cover in my talk both cursive models & printing types, if that is what you wd. like. Shall we call the talk "Italics in Calligraphy & Printing"?

My King Penguin is due to be out before the end of this month. It has many defects but I do think it cheap for 2/6. Jan Tschichold has given it as much care as if it were a five-guinea book. I hope your students won't get enthusiastic about copperplate through it!

All good wishes
Yours sincerely
Alfred Fairbank

ALFRED FAIRBANK Calligrapher and founder of the Society of Italic Handwriting.

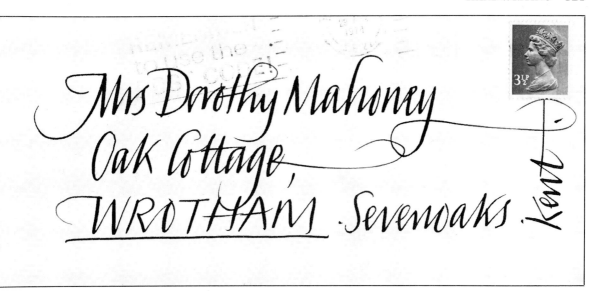

Top: IEUAN REES Calligrapher and letterer in stone, wood and slate.

Above left: SHEILA DONALDSON-WALTERS Illustrator and calligrapher.

Above: ALFRED FAIRBANK Calligrapher.

Left: GORDON RANSOM Painter and Head of Graphic Design at St Martins School of Art, London.

THE WHITE HOUSE, NORTH END
Nr. HENLEY ON THAMES

Telephone:
Turville Heath
362

24 · X · 1971 ·

Dear Dorothy · When undergoing the painful process of hunting for something I could not find, I was rewarded by unearthing the enclosed. You will be pleased so am I. as you can guess. as well as being indeed sorry that you have been deprived of the sheet for so long. I am sorry but relieved.

IRENE WELLINGTON Calligrapher.

TOM BARNARD Platignum Pen Company
representative promoting italic handwriting in schools.

Platignum Schools Division

NOV · 14th78

PLATIGNUM PEN CO. LTD. SIX HILLS WAY STEVENAGE HERTS TEL: 2488

Dear Mrs. Mahoney. I enclose items as promised & hope you will find them satisfactory. I've included a selection of pens as it saves frequent changes of the different widths of nib.

Sincerely, Tom Barnard.

MEMORANDUM

Library

Telephone No.: KENSINGTON 6371
Telegraphic Address: VICALEUM, LONDON

Victoria & Albert Museum

South Kensington, S.W.7

30th July. 1951

MINISTRY OF
EDUCATION

Dear Mrs. Mahoney,

Many thanks for your letter: I have heard nothing further from Van Trigt; and there is just a possibility that I may be on leave (working at home) from Wed. of this week. But if the portfolio is brought over here, I shall ensure that it is properly looked after.

yours sincerely

James Wardrop

JAMES WARDROP Eminent renaissance palaeographer.

HEATHER CHILD Calligrapher, designer and writer.

HEATHER CHILD · MBE
SEVENTY · HEATH ROAD · PETERSFIELD · HAMPSHIRE · GU31 4EJ
Telephone: Petersfield 61724

10. V. 79

Dear Dorothy —
Many thanks for your p.c. inviting me to send you some photographs of my recent work for possible reproduction in your books. The fact is that almost all my recent work has been heraldic and

Thursday ii

UNION-CASTLE LINE

Dear Charlie,

There is very little to write about after a week spent on board. The subtle monotony of our slow progress becomes after a few days quite agreeable when the cold grey swell of English seas give place to the rich Mediterranean blue & comparative calm of the tropical ocean. My head was swimming with dizzyness the first two days, numbers retired into the bowels of the ship to nurse their anguish in solitude but I was not one of these, & indeed, when at the end of the second day bad weather came & the ship pitched & tossed & rolled I felt exhilerated as I did on the memorable Channel crossing we had together. Each day the weather is noticeably hotter; at the start it was cold & grew more chilly on the second day when the wind whistled along the decks blowing out clothes & making trousers flah furiously as one was pushed or pulled about by it. The few who appeared on deck were despondent with apprehension for late on the previous evening we passed three cargo ships, each within a few miles of each other, blazing furiously,

EDWARD BAWDEN Artist, mural painter and illustrator. A letter written to my husband after the beginning of the War.

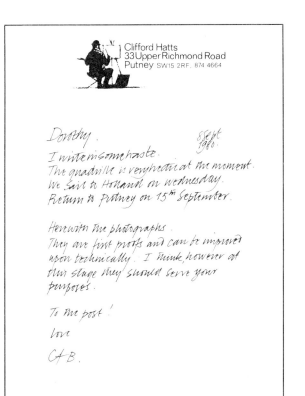

Clifford Hatts
33 Upper Richmond Road
Putney SW15 2RF. 874 4664

Dorothy.   8 Sept
                                            1980.
I write in some haste.
The quadrille is very hectic at the moment.
We sail to Holland on Wednesday.
Return to Putney on 15th September.

Herewith the photographs.
They are first proofs and can be improved
upon technically. I think, however at
this stage they should serve your
purposes.

To the post!

Love

C.H.

23 Castrille. Claremont Rd.
     Bath Avn

                    May

dear Dorothy
Here is a small package — for
the moment! The 3 Xeroxes I
am having proper
shines taken of x
they will follow! I
still quite like the
V+A booklet ones —
at least they do still
show what I am
trying to do. wh. is
to make the words
BE what they mean

Please forgive the very scrappy
      sheet —— I'll send

Left: CLIFFORD HATTS Graphic designer and former Head of Design Group, BBC Television.

Right: ANN HECHLE Calligrapher.

From Edward Johnston's notes on 'Freedom'

'Within the limits of our Craft we cannot have too much freedom ; for too much fitting and planning makes a work lifeless, and it is conceivable that in the finest work Rules are concealed, and that, for example, a MS might be most beautiful without ruled lines and methodical arrangement.'

INDEX

ABC

General Type

A rapidly written Penman's Initial Letter, untouched (like ordy. MS.) except for filling in of natural hollows.
As in ordy. formal MS. the thicks are markedly contrasted with the thins
& all natural angles are left (wh. further enhances this contrast) (& see Construction)

ABC

E.G. **A** or **A** NOT→ **A** or **A**

Construction { Note: 3 widths of stroke to be kept quite distinct & contrasting.

THICK STEMS Built up
THIN STEMS thick stroke
Serifs or Hairlines thin stroke

EARLY abt. 10th. C. (& after) rather Roman in type & plain **THICKER**

↑ less abrupt curve than in later forms

LATER abt. 12th c. (& after) rather more curved & tending to be ornament **AB**

↑ Abrupt back curve

In the 14th C. (& after) they got v. heavy (& frequently unreadable)

DP &c.

The Early more Roman Type makes the best practice & you can introduce the Round
D E G H M U forms made with less abrupt, or with slimmer, curves E.G.

EE match (& can be used EVEN in the same word)

Remember to keep { All sizes of letters on the same p. approximately equal in weight (This is the normal & the best plan for studying possibilities)

EE also match, but in a later type

But when a contrast in Letter weight is required (or, "necessary") let the contrast be very marked